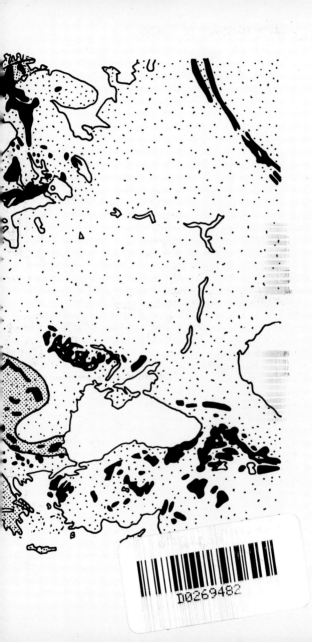

D0269482

LETTS POCKET GUIDE TO

ROCKS & MINERALS

The most common rocks and minerals
of Europe described and illustrated in
colour

E. Fejer, S. Frampton, C. Fitzsimons

Front cover illustration: Bornite and Chalcopyrite

This edition first published 1991
by Charles Letts & Co Ltd
Diary House, Borough Road,
London SE1 1DW

'Letts' is a registered trademark of
Charles Letts (Scotland) Ltd

This edition produced under licence by
Malcolm Saunders Publishing Ltd, London
Editorial assistance by Pamela Forey

© 1991 this edition Atlantis Publications Ltd

All rights reserved. No part of this publication
may be reproduced, stored in a retrieval system,
or transmitted, in any form or by any means,
electronic, mechanical, photocopying, recording
or otherwise without the prior written permission of
the copyright holder.

British Library Cataloguing in Publication Data
Fejer, Eva
    Rocks and minerals.
    1. Minerals. Rocks
    I. Title   II. Frampton, Steve   III. Fitzsimons, Cecilia
    533

    ISBN 1 85238 117 5

Contents

Introduction

This is a book for those who want to be able to identify the rocks or minerals that they come across, rocks exposed in river valleys or in quarries, showing up where new roads are cut through hills or when new houses are built; it is for those who are curious about the stone of which their house is built, or the minerals from which the rocks are formed. It is also for those people who want to be able to identify pieces of crystal or mineral fragments they might find on the shore, on old mine tips or even in the soil in their back garden.

Many people who do not have the time or opportunity to make a close study of them would still like to be able to identify these rocks and minerals. We have described and illustrated the most frequently occurring rocks and made a selection of the over two thousand known minerals. The names used for minerals in this book are those used in reference books but gemstone names, where these are different, are also indicated where relevant.

How to use this book

We have divided the book into two sections, **rocks** and **minerals**. The rock section is further divided into **sedimentary**, **igneous** and **metamorphic rocks**, a division which reflects how the rocks were formed.

In the mineral section, the minerals are arranged in order of hardness (see Fig. 1) rather than by colour, because the hardness of a mineral is characteristic, whereas colour is very variable.

Important: Since descriptions of rocks and minerals involve many unavoidable technical terms which are unfamiliar to the lay reader, we have introduced a detailed *Glossary* on pages 14–15 and the back endpapers contain illustrations of mineral forms and crystal types.

Guide to identification

First decide whether you are looking at a rock or a mineral. Rocks are made of minerals, so if you are looking at a huge piece of stone in a quarry or in a road cutting or at a cliff, you are looking at a rock. If, however, you are looking at the constituents of the rock, or at a group of obvious crystals, or at an ore, for example, then you are looking at a mineral.

Rocks

A map showing the distribution of the three kinds of rocks can be found on the front endpaper of this book. Fig. 3 (page 13) illustrates where rocks occur.

 SEDIMENTARY ROCKS are formed by the accumulation of sediments from weathering and erosion and deposition of existing rocks. They may consist of minerals, rock debris or organic matter. They have a layered appearance, from the accumulation and compression of the sediments from which they are formed. They may be soft, like clays, or hard like limestones. The layers may be thick and massive, as in some sandstones (18) or close together as in shales (19). Texture may be fine, as in chalk (20), grainy as in sandstones, or pebbly as in conglomerates (16).

 IGNEOUS ROCKS are formed when magma solidifies. When it solidifies above the surface the rocks are known as extrusive igneous rocks. When the magma solidifies beneath the surface the rocks formed are known as intrusive igneous rocks; they are often squeezed into cracks and intruded between layers of older rocks. In appearance, igneous rocks are crystalline (although the crystals may be too small to see with the naked eye); they may be uniformly grainy in texture, especially when the crystals are tiny, as in basalts (35), or granular, as in granites (28). The crystals may be arranged in zones but the rocks never present a layered appearance.

 METAMORPHIC ROCKS are rocks that have been altered from their original form by changes in heat and pressure at depth inside the earth. These changes may occur during folding and Fault movement or baked by contact with magma. Metamorphic rocks are especially common in mountain-building areas; they may be formed from igneous, sedimentary or even existing metamorphic rocks. Contact metamorphic rocks from a zone around an intrusion of magma, where the molten rock has come into contact with the surrounding rocks. The appearance of a metamorphic rock depends on its origin.

Minerals

The minerals in this book are divided into five subsections, according to their hardness, from the softest to the hardest. Hardness symbols at the top of the page provide a quick guide to the five sections. Hardness is a measure of the resistance of a mineral to scratching and the degree of hardness of each mineral is given in the colour panel at the top of the page, (as 1–2, for example) according to *Mohs' Scale of Hardness*.

In this scale, ten minerals are arranged in order, so that each one will scratch those lower in the scale. This scale is widely used as an indicator of hardness. Minerals with a hardness of less than 2 are so soft that they can be scratched with a fingernail; minerals with a hardness of 2–3 can be scratched with a copper coin; minerals with a hardness of 3–6 with a quality steel penknife; minerals with a hardness of 6–7 will not scratch glass and those with a hardness over 7 will scratch glass. The *Mohs' Scale of Hardness* is given below, and symbols for the five sections in Fig. 1.

Mohs' Scale of Hardness

Fig. 1 Key to hardness symbols

Hardness 1–2

Minerals which can be scratched with a fingernail

Hardness 2–3

Minerals which can be scratched with a copper coin and will scratch a fingernail

Hardness 3–6

Minerals which can be scratched by a quality steel penknife, and will scratch fingernails and copper coins

Hardness 6–7

Minerals which will not scratch glass, but will scratch steel blades, copper coins and fingernails

Hardness 7–10

Minerals which will scratch glass and all the other materials listed above

10

Density

An additional aid to identification of minerals is provided by the figure giving density, shown in the colour band at the top of the page. Density or specific gravity (S.G.) is the relative density of a mineral compared with water, which has a specific gravity of 1. The average for all known minerals is 2.7. Minerals with S.G. of 1.5 to 2.9 feel light in the hand; 3 to 3.9 moderately heavy; 4.0 to 6.0 heavy, and above 6.0 very heavy. With experience, specific gravity can be very useful for field identification. Remember to obtain a pure specimen for a meaningful result.

Fig. 2 Specimen page (mineral)

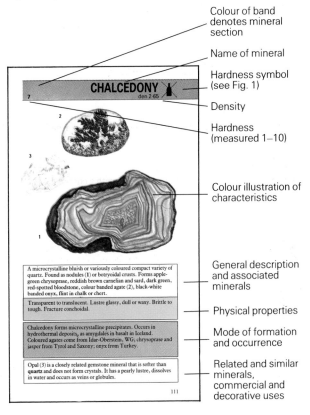

Colour of band denotes mineral section

Name of mineral

Hardness symbol (see Fig. 1)

Density

Hardness (measured 1–10)

Colour illustration of characteristics

General description and associated minerals

Physical properties

Mode of formation and occurrence

Related and similar minerals, commercial and decorative uses

Text from specimen page:

CHALCEDONY

7   den 2·65

A microcrystalline bluish or variously coloured compact variety of quartz. Found as nodules (1) or botryoidal crusts. Forms apple-green chrysoprase, reddish brown carnelian and sard, dark green, red-spotted bloodstone, colour banded agate (2), black-white banded onyx, flint in chalk or chert.

Transparent to translucent. Lustre glassy, dull or waxy. Brittle to tough. Fracture conchoidal.

Chalcedony forms microcrystalline precipitates. Occurs in hydrothermal deposits, as amygdales in basalt in Iceland. Coloured agates come from Idar-Oberstein, WG, chrysoprase and jasper from Tyrol and Saxony; onyx from Turkey.

Opal (3) is a closely related gemstone mineral that is softer than quartz and does not form crystals. It has a pearly lustre, dissolves in water and occurs as veins or globules.

111

Making a positive identification

Once you have decided whether you are looking at a rock or a mineral, you can turn to the pages on which they are described and illustrated. Four boxes of text on each page provide information which make positive identification possible. The first two boxes provide details of the characteristic features and physical properties of the particular rock or mineral; the third box provides details of mode of formation and occurrence; the fourth box, details of similar rocks or minerals and any commercial uses.

Characteristic features and physical properties

Rocks: The colour and mineral content of the rocks are described in the first box on each page, together with its structure, particle size, presence of fossils etc. The second box contains details of its texture, bedding (where relevant), lustre etc.

Minerals: The colour(s) and form of the minerals are described in the first box on each page, together with any other minerals with which this one is associated. Minerals often occur together in characteristic associations. The form of a mineral may vary from crystalline to massive, botryoidal or incrusting etc; *for an explanation of these terms see the illustrations on the back endpapers of the book.*

The second box contains details of the physical properties which are always used in distinguishing minerals. The terms are all explained in the glossary on pages 14–15.

Mode of formation and occurrence

The mode of formation of the rock or mineral is described in the third box, together with some of the most well-known or important localities in which it occurs. Abbreviations of countries and places used in the text are given on page 124.

Similar rocks and minerals

In the fourth box there is a variety of information. On some pages, some of the similar rocks or minerals with which this one might be confused are indicated. On others, minerals in which the similarity is in internal structure, rather than in external appearance, may be described. Also included here are details of commercial uses, or use as decorative or gemstones.

Less common rocks and minerals

On some pages a different layout has ben adopted, where several rocks or minerals have been described and illustrated on the same page. These are generally less common or less likely to be encountered than the featured rocks and minerals.

Now you are ready to use this book. It is designed to fit into your pocket, so take it with you on your next trip and don't forget to tick your sightings on the checklist provided with the index.

Fig. 3 Where rocks occur

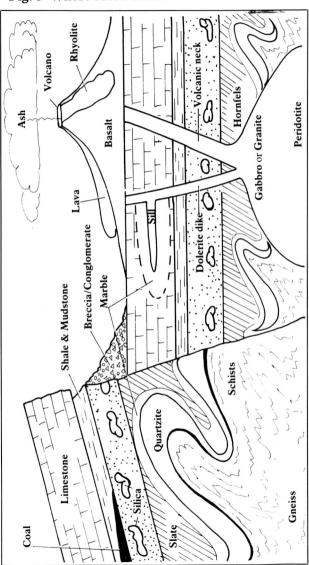

Glossary of terms

Mineral forms and crystal types are illustrated on the endpapers at the back of the book.

Accessory mineral Non-essential components found in small amounts in igneous rocks.

Alteration product The consequence of weathering, erosion and diagenesis.

Amygdale A gas cavity in a volcanic mineral, filled with calcite, quartz or zeolites.

Batholith A large intrusive igneous body.

Bedding The type of layering in sedimentary rocks.

Clast A fragment or grain in sedimentary rocks.

Cleavage The tendency of some minerals to break along one or more regular directions due to the structural arrangement of the atoms. The angle between such directions can often be diagnostic.

Concretion An irregular mass, often spherical, of locally cemented material found in sedimentary rocks.

Contact metamorphism The baking of rocks in contact with underground intrusions of hot magma.

Current bedding Inclined beds that are the product of wind or water currents.

Density The mass per unit volume of a substance (Specific Gravity).

Diagenesis Changes that take place after burial.

Dike An intrusive, usually thin and vertical sheet of igneous rock, which cuts across other rocks.

Double refraction The ability of a mineral to bend incident light rays in different directions within its crystals, causing double images to be seen, e.g. calcite.

Druse A rock surface, usually in a cavity, coated with crystals.

Ductile Applied to metals, the ability to be drawn into thin threads.

Erosion The physical disintegration of rocks due to wind, water and ice.

Fault A fracture in the earth's crust.

Fold Plastic deformation of rock strata.

Form The shape of a mineral.

Fracture The random way in which a mineral breaks. Ways include conchoidal (like a shell); earthy (like clay); hackly (with jagged edges); splintery (with needle-like fibres); uneven (with an irregular surface).

Gangue The minerals of no value in an ore vein.

Geode A rock concretion, usually rounded, often hollow and lined with crystals.

Habit The shape of a crystal.

Hydrothermal processes Geological processes involving heated water associated with igneous activity.

Lava Molten rock reaching the surface of the earth, often rapidly cooled and fine-grained.

Lustre The manner in which the surface of a substance responds to light.

Magma Molten rock beneath the surface of the earth.

Malleable Can be hammered into thin sheets.

Mantle Zone between the earth's crust and the iron-nickel core.

Metamorphism Changes in a rock caused by heat and pressure immediately below the surface, the level of which give the **metamorphic grade.**

Oolite Spherical grains of calcite, 1 mm/$\frac{1}{32}$ in diameter, which build limestones.

Ore A mineral which is present in large enough quantities to warrant its mining and refining.

Parting A smooth fracture in minerals, similar to cleavage.

Pegmatite A very coarse plutonic rock, usually similar to granite in composition.

Periglacial Processes acting at the edge of a glacier.

Phenocryst A mineral of large dimensions compared to the average grain size of an igneous rock.

Pillow lava Lava suddenly cooled underwater.

Placer An accumulation of dense economically valued material in rivers.

Plutonic rock An igneous rock, often coarse-grained, occurring in a deep-seated igneous intrusion.

Porphyritic igneous rocks These have a distinctive texture where larger crystals are surrounded by a fine-grained crystalline or glassy ground mass

Schistosity Parallel layering of micas in metamorphic rocks.

Secondary minerals Minerals formed by the alteration of pre-existing minerals.

Sectile Can be cut by a knife.

Shield Large old stable continental basement.

Sill A horizontal sheet of intrusive rock injected between layers of sedimentary or metamorphic rocks.

Streak The colour of the powder produced by rubbing a mineral on a piece of white unglazed porcelain.

Twinned crystals. Two or more crystals intergrown with a definite relationship between them.

Ultramafic/Ultrabasic rocks Rocks rich in Iron minerals and low in silica.

Vein A more or less upright deposit of minerals that cuts across the rocks around it.

Vesicle A once gas-filled cavity in an igneous rock.

Volcano A vent in the earth's crust through which magma, gases, ashes etc. escape to the surface.

Weathering The *in situ* disintegration of a rock due to the weather.

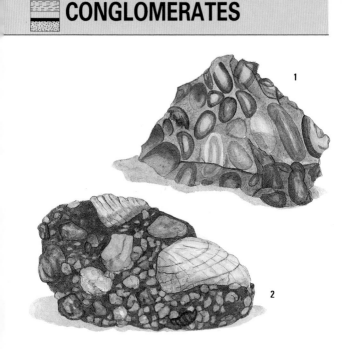

Colour variable. Composed of well rounded pebbles to boulders of quartz, chert (**1**), flint and other rock fragments. Pebbles are normally cemented with silica or calcite, and iron oxides may be present. Tillite (**2**) is cemented with clay minerals.

Hard, resistant rocks which may be loosely consolidated. Texture rough, pebbles often aligned in the same direction. Tillite pebbles often scratched and very variable in size.

Beach deposits or rich gravels laid down in fast moving water. Often found above unconformities. Pudding Stone is found in S. Eng. and Lucerne, Switz., other conglomerates are widespread. Tillites are deposited by glaciers and Recent tillite is widespread as a surface deposit in Northern Europe.

Conglomerates have rounded pebbles, tillites more angular, scratched ones and **breccia** fragments are sharply angular. **Sandstones** are less coarse.

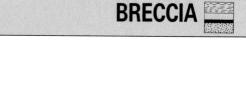

Colour variable. Composed of sharply angular fragments of many rock types, cemented in a fine- or medium-grained matrix of silica, calcite, clay or limonite.

Hardness varies depending on cementing media and rock fragments. Texture rough where the rock breaks around the larger rock fragments. Fossils and bedding rare.

Formed from scree material, in landslides and cave-ins. Fault breccias occur during folding and movements of the earth's crust. Fragments are angular because the breccia forms near where the old rocks break up. Widespread throughout Europe. Common in limestone regions.

Coarse angular fragments, often of same rock, are characteristic. Breccias do not contain volcanic material as do agglomerates. Limited use as building and paving stones.

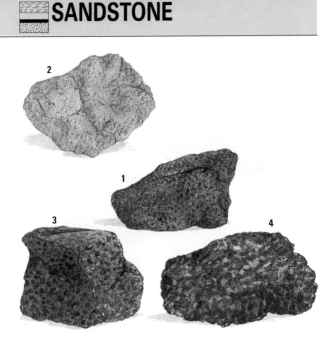

Colour variable, grey, brown, yellowish, reddish, determined by type, amount and colour of cement. Contains rounded or angular quartz grains which are cemented by clays or by silica, calcite, hematite (ferruginous sandstone, **1**), limonite (brownstone) or glauconite (greensand, **2**). May contain fossils.

Hardness variable, but very hard if cemented by silica. Forms ridges in the landscape between softer rocks. Often massive with current bedding and ripple marks. Texture even. Porous.

Formed in shallow waters as beach and delta deposits or from desert sands. Widespread throughout Europe, e.g. Fontainebleau quartzite in France, Alpine molasse (Switz., N. Italy), glauconite sandstones (Wales, Scand.), arkose (Vosges, France; Scand.), greywackes (Rhine valley; N. Appenines, Italy).

Arkose (**3**) is rich in feldspar. Greywacke (**4**) is an impure sandstone with fragments of various rocks. **Quartzite** contains 95% quartz. Useful building stones and as oil reservoirs.

CLAYS & SHALES

Colour grey to dark grey, brown, reddish, buff, yellow or dark green, depending on the presence of iron oxides and/or organic matter. These rocks consist of fine particles, very fine in soft clays and hard mudstones, gritty in siltstones. Minerals include a little quartz, feldspar and mica.

Massive or finely laminated, compact rocks. Fossils, ripple-marks, suncracks etc. are often abundant. Clays are soft and plastic, mudstones are hard and may break up when wet.

Sedimentary rocks deposited under marine or fresh water conditions: gritty siltstones in shallower water, fine-grained shales in deeper waters. Found with sandstones and limestones. Widespread, e.g. Kupferschiefer Shale found from Poland to England, Tertiary Piedmontese Basin Marl of Italy.

Clay (1) is plastic. Marl (2) contains pyrite, gypsum and calcite. Siltstones (3) are gritty and shales (4) are laminated. **Mudstones** are hard and massive.

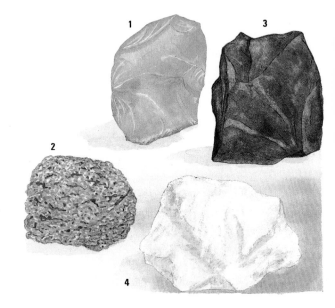

White, grey or yellowish, massive rocks. May be stained black, brown or reddish with impurities (iron oxides, quartz or clay). Composed of calcite and/or aragonite, occasionally dolomite. May contain silica, chert, hematite or limonite, veins of calcite and other minerals. Fossils rare.

Fine-grained, dense, massive rock, often with large scale bedding. Fracture conchoidal. Bubbles in cold dilute acid. Dissolves in water to reform in caves, stalagtites, hot springs.

Calcareous mudstones are chemical deposits, e.g. Solenhofen, Bavaria. Tufa and travertine form stalagtites/mites in caves and hot springs, as in Tivoli, Italy. In dolomite, water replaces calcite with magnesium, as in the Dolomites, Italy. Chalk deposited in clear deep seas is found in N. France; Eng.

Calcareous mudstones (1) are fine grained, travertine (2) is spongy. Dolomite (3) only bubbles slowly in cold dilute acid. Chalk (4) is a very pure limestone and lacks bedding.

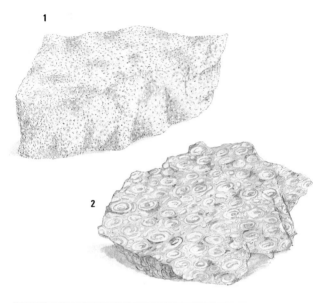

Colour white, yellow or brown. Usually composed of calcite and/or aragonite with some silica, hematite or dolomite. Composed of masses of spherical grains cemented by a crystalline matrix. Oolitic grains (**1**) are 1–2mm ($\frac{1}{32}$–$\frac{1}{16}$in) in diameter, and resemble cod roe. Pisolitic (**2**) grains are larger and pea-like.

Relatively soft, massive rocks which bubble when treated with cold dilute acid. Often current bedded. They contain some fossils.

Formed by calcite deposited in layers around shell and sand fragments rolling on the bed in warm shallow seas, as in Bahama Banks and hot springs today. Grade into other limestones and sandstones: Modern Pisolites at Vichy, France; Karlsbad, Cz. and Lower Carboniferous Oolites of England and Germany.

Distinguished from other limestones by fish-roe or pea-like appearance. **Sandstones** do not react with acid. These are attractive building stones.

Colour white, grey or yellow; brownish if impure. Composed of numerous assorted fossil fragments set in a fine-grained limestone matrix. Main minerals are calcite and aragonite, derived from the fossils; the rocks may also contain chert, silica, pyrite, dolomite and locally bitumen.

Hardness varies, when weathered they may be crumbly, pitted or pock-marked. Bedding is common. Large scale reef structures may be preserved. Bubbles in cold dilute acid.

Deposited as accumulations of shelled creatures and reef building organisms in clear, shallow waters. Interbedded with other limestones, sandstones, shales and mudstones. Widespread: Carinthia, Aus.; Branzi, Bergamo, It.; the Permian of Italian Tyrol and the extensive Carboniferous limestone.

Numerous fossil fragments distinguish this from other limestones and it is the best source of shelled fossils. Indiana limestone is an important building stone.

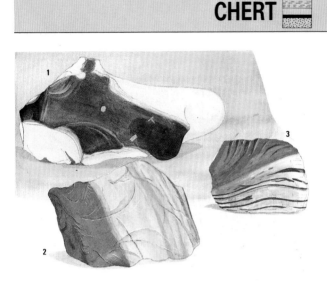

Colour white, grey to black (flint, **1**), with yellow, brown (**2**), green and red (jasper, **3**) varieties. Occurs as nodules or as masses up to 275 metres (900ft) thick. May form wedge-like beds, interlayered with other sedimentary or volcanic deposits.

Texture dense, rough on weathered surface. Very hard and tough. Fracture conchoidal. As it resists erosion, it may stand out as nodules or massive outcrops on weathered surfaces.

Some chert seem to have formed by precipitation of silica from sea water, especially near volcanic regions. Others are the compacted and re-crystallized remains of minute animal or plant skeletons. In petrified wood, silica from ground water replaces the woody cells.

Identified by hardness and toughness. Because of these qualities, flint and chert were used by Early Man for the manufacture of weapons and implements and for striking fire.

COALS

Colour brown (peat, **1**), chocolate brown (lignite, **2**), black (bituminous coal, anthracite, **3**). May be porous, woody, well jointed or thinly laminated, depending on variety. Carbon is the chief constituent with some oxygen, hydrogen and sulphur. Occurs in layers or seams in other rocks.

Lustre dull (peat, lignite) to bright, glassy (anthracite). Dense. Fracture splintery to conchoidal. Plant remains may be visible in some coals.

Formed from decomposition of plant remains under very special conditions at high temperatures until a very high carbon content is achieved. Anthracite (best quality coal) is restricted to rocks of Carboniferous age. Mined throughout Europe. Peat is found in Ireland, West Germany, Poland and Denmark.

Important mineral fuel, until recently widely used for heating homes, now used in the iron and steel industry and in the manufacture of rubber and dyes.

IRONSTONES

Colour brown, red, green, yellow and blackish. These are sedimentary rocks containing at least 15% of iron minerals, including hematite, limonite, pyrite, magnetite, siderite, chamosite, glauconite. Calcite, dolomite and silica are also present.

Hardness and grain size variable, may be locally very hard or friable. They have fine and coarse beds, often current bedded, and may be oolitic. Organic remains are common.

Formed as chemical deposits in shallow waters. Interbedded with cherts, limestones and sandstones. Sedimentary ironstones are found in Alsace-Lorraine, France; Luxembourg; Westphalia, W. Germany and Sardinia, Italy.

Many ironstones are mined commercially for iron ore.

Colour white to yellow when pure; red, brown and grey if impure. Consists of an aggregate of aluminium hydroxides, including gibbsite, bochmite, diaspore and cliachite. Iron oxides and bitumen may also be present.

Very soft, earthy, clayey and fragile. May be oolitic or pisolitic, when brown concretions are surrounded by a yellow or grey matrix. Streak white.

A residual deposit formed in tropical conditions by the weathering and leaching of rocks rich in aluminium. Alumina is concentrated following the removal of carbonate and silica. Found in Ariege, France; Italy; Naxos, Greece; Yugoslavia, Hungary and the Urals, USSR.

Pisolitic structure, softness and very high aluminium content are characteristic. **Limestones** react with acid, **sandstones** contain quartz.

VOLCANOCLASTIC ROCKS

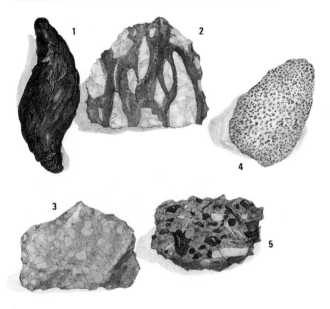

Bombs (1)
Bombs are dark brown, green or black lumps of lava, shaped and hardened as they fly in air.

Volcanic Breccia (2)
Composed of bombs and other angular rock fragments, cemented by volcanic dust.

Tuff (3)
Grey fine-grained, wind-blown volcanic dust. Often layered or containing pea-sized glassy grains. Found with lavas on Vesuvius, Italy. Also found in Greece, Turkey, Germany.

Pumice (4)
White to grey, vesicular and sponge-like. Formed from acid frothy lava, expelled from volcanoes under or near water. So lightweight it floats. Found on the Lipari Is., Italy and in Iceland. Used for insulation and soft abrasives.

Ignimbrite (5)
Light grey to brown, vesicular glass. Deposited from clouds of extremely hot gas and ash, ejected from volcanoes. It rushes downhill causing great devastation. Notably at Mt. Pelée, Martinique. Building stone.

27

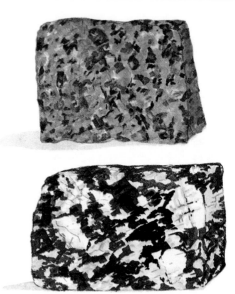

Colour varies from white, grey, to pink or reddish, depending on which feldspar is present and on its proportion to the dark minerals. Potash feldspars and quartz account for about 70% of the rock. Minor constituents include mica and hornblende, with apatite, topaz, garnet, hematite, zircon, and magnetite.

Fairly coarse-grained in texture, with large twinned feldspar phenocrysts. Graphic granite is a special intergrowth of quartz and feldspar, perthite of albite and potash feldspar.

Formed by slow cooling and crystallization of magma at depth in the continents, forming huge block jointed domes. Often forms sharp weather-resistant crags. Occurs at Mt. Blanc and Pyrenees, France; Aar-Gotthard, Switz.; Baveno, Predazzo and Sardinia, It., and UK, Port., WG. Very widespread.

There are many varieties of granite. It is a valuable ornamental and building stone, used rough or as polished slabs. The powdered rock has been used as fertilizer.

Colour light but variable because of uneven distribution of minerals present. Essential constituents similar to those of granite and syenite: quartz, feldspar (orthoclase, albite, microcline), mica, titanite, hornblende. May contain tourmaline, topaz, apatite, spodumene and many others.

Very coarse-grained in texture, unevenly granular. Individual crystals may be several feet long, growing inwardly from dyke walls, or into drusy cavities found in pegmatite bodies.

Formed under pressure at high temperatures by the rapid crystallization of minerals from fluids and gasses escaping from cooling silica-rich magma. Occurs as dykes cutting across parent rock or as irregular masses. Found in many localities including Como, It., Cornwall, Eng., Kola Peninsula, USSR.

Recognized by large size of crystals. The source of many economic minerals such as **mica** (an insulating material), **feldspars** (used in ceramics and glassmaking), and of gems.

Colour shades of grey, yellow, pink to deep red; the fine-grained volcanic equivalent of granite, high in silica. Contains mostly light-coloured minerals, also brown or dark green biotite, hornblende, a little magnesite, opal, topaz. Some alignment of crystals occurs in direction of lava flow.

Texture partly glassy, compact, with small crystals in glassy groundmass; may also be porous, brittle or spongy as in pumice. Flow structures and banding may be common.

Formed by rapid cooling when a viscous magma of granitic composition nears the surface or erupts at the surface. Occurs as lava flows, dykes, sills and in contact zones of large intrusions. Very abundant in Tuscany and on Lipari Isles, Italy; also seen in Iceland, Hungary and Romania.

When compact and devitrified it may be confused with **sandstone**. Quartz porphyry is a very old rhyolite. Rhyolite is used in chemical washing processes.

OBSIDIAN

Colour smoky grey, dark green to black or may be streaked brownish red and black. A relatively rare glassy igneous rock where lava cooled too fast to crystallize but may contain tiny fragments of granite minerals. Alters and devitrifies. Pitchstone is partially decomposed obsidian.

Transparent to translucent with tiny inclusions causing cloudiness. Texture and lustre glassy. Very marked conchoidal fracture. Very hard, scratches window glass.

Formed from very thick silica-rich lava flows, a sign of recent geologically active continental volcanoes. Obsidian is very common on the Lipari Isles, Italy, and around Landmannalaugar, Iceland.

One of the most easily recognized rocks, once highly valued by primitive peoples. Free rounded glassy pebbles are collected and fashioned into jewellery.

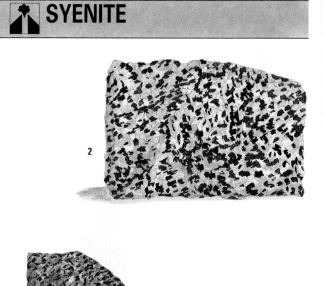

Colour variable, pinkish, reddish (**1**), grey (**2**), or even violet depending on proportion of feldspars to dark minerals like biotite or amphiboles. About 70% of rock consists of potash and plagioclase feldspars. May also contain muscovite, apatite, corundum, titanite, zircon and nepheline.

Texture medium-grained with occasional pegmatite zones. Often occurs as a quartz-poor border zone of granite bodies. It exhibits block jointing similar to granite.

Much less common than granite, occurring as small intrusions or dykes. Origin still controversial. Syenite areas well-known for their mineral content include those at Aswan, Egypt; the Oslo region and South and Central Norway, and the Black Forest, Germany.

Contains little or no free quartz, otherwise similar in appearance to **granite**. Used locally as a building stone.

Colour grey, dark grey, sometimes greenish to brownish grey. Contains even less quartz than syenite. Feldspars, biotite, amphiboles and pyroxenes account for 50% of rock. Other minerals present include apatite, zircon, titanite, magnetite, ilmenite. May also contain diopside, garnets and spinel.

Texture medium- to coarse-grained, porphyritic, with crystals of twinned feldspar, hornblende or biotite. Some feldspar is aligned in bands in the direction of the original magma flow.

Occurs as stocks, sills, dykes. Formed by slow deep-seated cooling of magma richer in iron and magnesium than granite. Uneven weathering emphasizes flow banding and alignment. Occurs in Haute Savoie, France; Sondrio, Itraly; Thuringia and Sassonia, WG; Romania, Sweden and Finland.

A very durable, easily polished ornamental and building stone, but little used because of its drab colour. Erosion occasionally creates shapes similar to those in **granite**.

♣ GABBRO

Colour dark grey, greenish black, reddish, sometimes paler or mottled depending on minerals present. Like basalt, it is essentially composed of plagioclase feldspar, pyroxene, amphibole and olivine. May contain a little quartz, biotite, rutile, magnetite, titanite, corundum, apatite and spinel.

A coarse-grained rock with porphyritic texture. Usually massive but may appear to have a layered or orbicular structure. Weathers and erodes more rapidly than granites.

Formed at great depth by slow cooling and crystallization from fluid magma low in silica. Occurs as sheet- or saucer-shaped intrusions, occasionally associated with important mineral deposits. Well represented in the Swiss and Italian Alps, e.g. Zermatt. Also Corsica, Greece, Turkey, and Harz Mts., WG.

Diabase is a less porphyritic, tough variety of gabbro used as road metal, railroad ballast and roofing material. Gabbro is a main source of **olivine** used as lining in blast furnaces.

1

Colour dark grey to black. A fine-grained compact volcanic rock with a low silica content. Essential minerals are plagioclase feldspar, pyroxene (augite) and olivine, with a little magnetite, ilmenite, amphibole (hornblende). Vesicular cavities (1) are usually filled with a zeolite and/or quartz.

As basaltic lava thickens on cooling, trapped gases expand and cavities (vesicles) form. These fill with minerals precipitated from volcanic gases and fluids.

Formed from massive lava flows thousands of metres thick covering vast areas, including ocean floors. Recently erupted lavas in Iceland show different modes of solidification. Basalts also occur in Greenland, Scotland, on Etna in Sicily and in the Canary Islands.

Identified by its dark colour, weight and vesicular structure. Basalt is the fine-grained equivent of a **gabbro**. Used for road paving, crushed for road and railway ballast.

Colour dull green to black, yellowish green (dunite), with a mottled appearance. Composed of olivine, pyroxene, amphibole, or just dunite and pyroxenite. May contain chromite, biotite, magnetite, pyrope, spinel. Serpentine and talc when present are alteration products.

Texture medium- to coarse-grained. Hardness is variable depending on degree of alteration. Weathering changes colour and surface becomes pitted.

Formed at depth by slow cooling and crystallization of a very basic magma. Occurs as dykes, sills, large or small stocks. May be stratified. Found in the Lizard Complex of Cornwall, England; the Urals, USSR; the immense Bushveld complex of South Africa.

Peridotite is a source of valuable minerals such as chromite, native platinum, **talc** and **chrysotile**. Diamonds are mined from kimberlite, a mica peridotite.

Diabase (1)

Highly variable in grain size, texture and colour, but usually black, dark grey, green or black & white. Found in dykes and sills in Scot. and WG. Hard and withstands crushing, used for concrete, road and rail ballast. May be polished.

Quartz Porphyry (2)

Acid rock composed of quartz, orthoclase and biotite. Found as lava flows, sills and dykes. Light grey-pink, porphyritic with quartz phenocrysts. Biellese to Varesotta, It.; Lunganese, Switz.; Sassonia, Westphalia, WG.

Andesite (3)

Brown, green, purple or dark grey. Porphyritic with large crystals of plagioclase, biotite, hornblende and augite in a fine ground matrix. Formed in lava flows and dykes during mountain building in Tauro, Tur.; Transylvania, Rom.; Padua, It.

Trachyte (4)

Usually grey, may be tan, pink or white. Fine-grained with lath-like feldspar crystals in near parallel alignment. In lava flows and narrow dykes of basalt volcanoes. Widespread in Hungary; Drachenfels, WG; Solfatara, Naples, It.

MARBLE

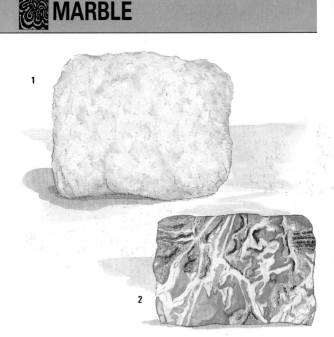

Colour normally white (**1**), but may be tinted black, green, yellow or brown, often blotchy or veined (**2**). Consists mainly of calcite, with some dolomite, hematite, serpentine, talc, epidote, diopside. Silicate minerals, when present, increase the hardness of marble.

Texture finely to coarsely granular, even-grained or sugary. Lustre soft glassy on fracture surfaces. Easily scratched by pocket knife.

Derived from fairly pure limestone by regional or contact metamorphism. In areas of metamorphic rocks, marble occurs interbedded with mica schist or gneiss. Found at Carrara, Liguria and in Tuscany, Italy; in the W. Italian Alps and in the Tyrol.

Quarried extensively as a building and/or ornamental stone. It is named for its colour or its place of origin. Polished slabs are used for pedestals, washbasins and tabletops.

Colour mid to dark grey, even black (from enclosed graphite and organic matter), green (from chlorite), red, purple, brown or yellow. Composed mainly of microscopic platy crystals of muscovite and chorite aligned to produce its distinct slaty foliation.

Texture dense, microscopic, with silky sheen, although garnet and andalusite may sometimes be visible. Splits readily into thin sheets. Easily scratched by pocket knife.

Formed by regional metamorphism from shale or mudstone under pressure. Occurs as steeply tilted outcrops with jagged or irregular outlines caused by weathering. Quarried in Barr Andlau, Vosges, France; N. Wales and the English Lake District; Orijarvi, Finland and several other places.

Readily recognized by its slaty appearance. Used for roofing slate, flagstones, blackboards and for flooring.

QUARTZITE

Colour white if only quartz is present, patchy grey to black, reddish or yellowish when other minerals are present. Accessory minerals include micas, potash and plagioclase feldspars, apatite, zircon, pyrite, magnetite, ilmenite, occasionally graphite, garnet and calcite.

Texture fine-grained, sometimes sugary. Structure foliated or schistose, depending on abundance of mica. May grade into quartz schist.

Widespread in metamorphic rocks derived from sandstone, mudstone, greywacke, jasper and flint, but also formed from metamorphosed pegmatite. Often masses of quartzite are impregnated with iron minerals. Occurs in the Highlands of Scotland and at many other localities.

One of the hardest and most resistant rocks of all. Often used for flooring or facing, also used in the glass and ceramics industries.

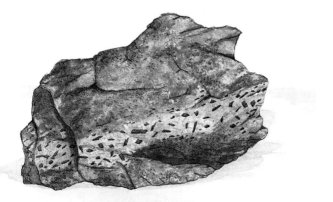

Colour variable, pink, brown, violet or green, also dark grey to black. May be spotted or knotted. Compact, massive. Often associated minerals alone are visible. These include albite, actinolite, garnet, feldspar, apatite, axinite, cordierite, corundum, diopside, fluorite, spinel, quartz and others.

Texture dense, very compact. Lustre dull. Fracture splintery to conchoidal. Breaks into sharp angular pieces.

Formed by contact metamorphism of clayey sediments at high temperatures when the original constituents are recrystallized. Found in contact with or close to large deep-seated masses of igneous rock. Found at Barr Andlau, Vosges, France; Laachersee, West Germany; Oslo, Norway.

Recognized by the pattern of fracturing. Of minor use as crushed stone.

GNEISS

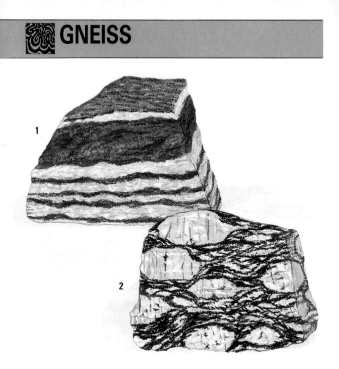

Colour generally light (grey, pink) with darker foliated bands. Consists of layers (**1**) or large eyes (augen gneiss, **2**), quartz and feldspar and narrower bands of well aligned biotite and hornblende associated with apatite, garnet, corundum, staurolite, andalusite, cordierite and titanite.

Texture uneven, granular and medium- to coarse-grained with more or less parallel alignment of minerals. Quartz-feldspar layers are hard, mica bands soft.

Formed by regional metamorphism, involving intensive folding and deformation, from deep-seated igneous rocks and from some sedimentary sandstones, conglomerates or shales. Widespread. Occurs in the Alps, at Mont Blanc, Monte Rosa and Monte Leone. Also in Scandinavia and in Spain and Portugal.

Nearly as resistant to erosion as **granite**. Occasionally still used as building stone. Demarcation between **schist** and gneiss is arbitrary.

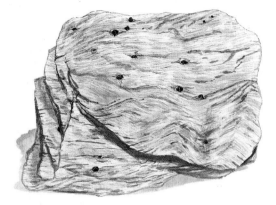

Colour silvery white, shades of grey, greenish or brownish. Alignment of thin plates of mica, chlorite or talc causes foliation. Contains mainly quartz, mica or chlorite, with apatite, tourmaline, zircon, garnet, magnetite, glaucophane, pyrite, kyanite, staurolite, epidote, cordierite and others.

Texture variable. Feltlike, fine- to coarse-grained, foliated (schistose) with "eyes" of accessory minerals. Lustre silky, sparkling from reflection of aligned platy minerals.

Formed by regional metamorphism from shale, sandstone, slate, rhyolite, basalt, at varying temperatures and pressures. Mica schist is found from the Alps to N. Scotland. Chlorite schist is found in the W. Alps and central Scotland. Talc schist occurs in C. and E. Alps, Pyrenees, Tuscany, It., and Sweden.

Recognized in the field by foliation, often in tilted or folded rocks. Locally used.

Phyllite (1)
Quartz, mica, chlorite and
graphite. Silvery green, fine-
grained with wavy schistosity.
Eastern Alps, Ardennes,
Rhineland Massif, Devon, Eng.
Locally used for roofing.

Amphibolite (2)
Basic. Amphiboles and
plagioclase with epidote, quartz,
garnet, mica. Dark green
speckled white. Massive altered
basalt lavas and tuffs. Extensive
in Valtellina and Orobian Alps,
It. Abundant in Norwegian
Baltic Shield.

Serpentinite (3)
Ultramafic; serpentine and
magnetite with talc and chlorite.
Variegated red-green, waxy,
coarse mottled with veining.
Alteration of peridote.
Widespread in Alps and Lizard
Complex, Eng. An ornamental
stone.

Mylonite (4)
Formed at low temperatures and
high pressure along lines of
tectonic movement. Massive,
compact, black, schistose and
fine-grained. Insubrica line in
central Alps.

Migmatite (1)
Layered mixture of dark schist or gneiss, and light granite. Inner zone of the aureole of large granite intrusions. Black Forest, WG, Finland.

Skarn (2)
Formed at granite-limestone contact. Calcite, pyroxene, garnet with metal sulphides. Coarse, dark, granoblastic. Fine source of many minerals. Sweden.

Granulite (3)
Orthoclase, plagioclase, quartz and garnet with pyroxene, kyanite, cordierite and sillimanite. Variable grain size and colour, granoblastic texture. Scandinavia.

Eclogite (4)
Dense, basic, high pressure product of pyroxene, garnet, with quartz, rutile, pyrite, kyanite, corundum. Zoned and speckled green, red. Coarse. Massive with garnet and pyroxene porphyroblasts. Western Alps, Norway, NW Scotland.

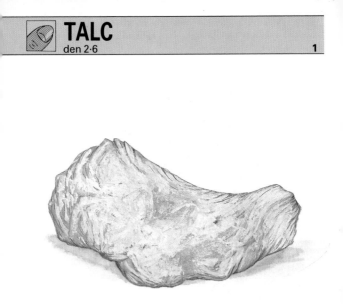

Talc (1) is pale green, greyish or white. Crystals are rare, monoclinic. Usually occurs as foliated or fine-grained masses, or in massive form (soapstone). Associated with actinolite, tremolite and magnesite.

Translucent. Lustre dull, pearly on the cleavage surface. Cleavage perfect, basal. It is soft, easily cut and feels soapy. Streak white to pale green.

Talc is formed from the metamorphic alteration of silicaceous dolomites (soapstone) or ultrabasic rocks like peridotite. It also forms along fault lines in magnesian-rich rocks. It is found in Styria, Austria; the Lizard Complex, Cornwall, England; Val Chisone, Piedmont and Orani, Sardinia, Italy.

Kaolinite (2) is similar, occurring as soft, plastic, earthy masses; it is the china clay for ceramics. Talc is used as a lubricant, electrical insulator and for talcum powder.

Colour bluish grey. The crystals are six-sided plates, easily bent and therefore often distorted. Also found as foliated masses, scales, rarely in granular form. Occurs with quartz, cassiterite, chalcopyrite; pyrite, scheelite and garnet, also with pyrite and barite.

Opaque. Lustre bright metallic. Cleavage perfect, parallel to plates. Feels greasy. Thin flakes are flexible but not elastic. Sectile. Molybdenite is soft and heavy.

Found in very high temperature veins, pegmatites and metamorphic deposits in limestone. Splendid crystals occur at Raade, Norway. Climax, Colorado, USA has produced 90% of world output. Smaller deposits are found in Cornwall, England; Bohemia; West Germany, Italy and Yugoslavia.

Distinguished from **graphite** by its bluish colour. Otherwise readily identified. Principal source of molybdenum. Used in alloys and as a temperature resistant dry lubricant.

Graphite (**1**) is iron black to steel grey in colour. Occurs as hexagonal, thin tabular crystals or more commonly in massive, foliated or earthy form.

Opaque. Lustre metallic to dull. Cleavage perfect, basal. It is flaky, soft and greasy and marks fingers and paper.

Graphite occurs in metamorphic schists and gneisses, in veins in igneous rocks and pegmatites. Occurs near Val Chisone, Italy; in Borrowdale, England; Bohemia; Bavaria, West Germany.

Graphite and diamond are both carbon minerals. Diamond is the hardest known mineral (10). Graphite is used for making fire-resistant crucibles for steel and in nuclear reactors.

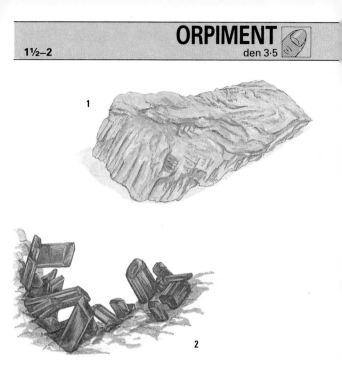

1

2

Lemon yellow or orange. Crystals are rare. Usually occurs in foliated form with thin flexible but not elastic flakes. Also occurs in granular (1) or fibrous forms or as earthy incrustations. Occurs with stibnite, cinnabar, calcite, arsenic, barite, gypsum and realgar.

Translucent to transparent. Lustre resinous, pearly on cleavages. Cleavage perfect basal as in mica. May be cut by a knife. Fairly heavy.

Occurs in hydrothermal veins and hot spring deposits. A common alteration product of arsenic minerals. Large mica-like crystals are found at Nagyag, Romania. Also occurs at Binnetal, Switzerland; Matra, Corsica; Sondrio and Tuscany, Italy. Orpiment tends to disintegrate on exposure to light and air.

Reddish-yellow realgar (2) decays to form orpiment and the two are often found together. **Sulphur** lacks the perfect cleavage of orpiment and **cinnabar** is heavier.

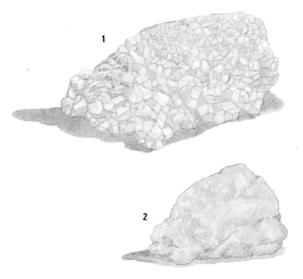

Colour pale lemon yellow when pure, otherwise greenish yellow, amber, brown, reddish, greyish. Crystals (**1**) are usually steep bipyramids (large crystals common in Italy), sometimes tabular. Also occurs in granular, fibrous or compact form (**2**) or as crusts. Often found with stibnite and cinnabar.

Transparent to translucent. Lustre greasy, resinous. Cleavage poor, basal and prismatic. Fracture conchoidal. Very brittle. Lightweight. Poor conductor of electricity.

Found in volcanic rocks. Mined deposits may have a sedimentary origin, formed by the decomposition of minerals like gypsum. Occurs throughout the Appenines, especially in Romagna and Sicily, Italy. The best crystals come from Agrigento, Sicily.

Unlikely to be mistaken for any other mineral. A fungicide and used by rubber and chemical industries. Crystals crack easily in warm hands, should be kept out of the sun and not handled.

Colour lead grey, black when tarnished. Crystals are stout or slender prisms grooved lengthwise, slightly twisted, with terminal faces. Commonly occurs as aggregates of needle-like crystals or in granular form or as radiating or columnar masses. Found with orpiment, calcite, realgar and galena.

Opaque. Lustre bright metallic. Cleavage perfect, parallel to grooves. Brittle. Fracture subconchoidal, slightly sectile. For a metallic mineral it is relatively lightweight.

Abundant in hydrothermal veins or hot spring deposits. Outstanding crystals occur at Kapnik, Romania and Rosia (Siena), Italy. Also found in central France; Como, Grosseto and Sardinia, Italy.

Identified by its slightly twisted crystals and light weight. The chief ore of antimony, widely used in industry. In ancient times it was used as a cosmetic preparation.

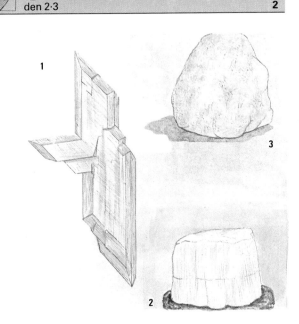

Colourless, white, grey, yellowish, brown or reddish. Occurs as tabular transparent crystals up to 90 cm (3 ft.) long, as swallowtail or spearhead twins, as cleavage fragments (selenite, **1**), fibrous or silky aggregates (satin spar, **2**) or as banded alabaster. Desert roses are rosette-like aggregates with sand grains.

Transparent. Lustre silky, on cleavage faces pearly. Perfect cleavage results in slightly flexible but inelastic fine flakes. Soft, can be scratched by fingernail.

Mainly found with anhydrite in sedimentary rocks and hydrothermal deposits. Loose crystals of selenite occur in clay beds of Pavia and Sicily, Italy. Massive beds occur in Paris Basin, France and Pisa, Italy. Desert roses are found in Tunisia and Morocco, swallowtail twins in Montmartre, Paris.

Anhydrite (**3**) occurs at depth and is converted to gypsum at the surface. Gypsum is softer than **muscovite** or **calcite**. It is used for plaster and cement, banded alabaster for carvings.

Colour bright red to brick red. Crystals are tabular or complex twins. Fine needles are very rare. It is usually massive (**1**) or occurs in granular form (**2**) or as earthy incrustations. Found with pyrite, marcasite, stibnite, opal, chalcedony, quartz, calcite and dolomite.

Translucent to transparent, massive varieties opaque. Lustre resinous to dull. Cleavage perfect, in three directions at 60° or 120°. Brittle, can be cut by knife. Fracture uneven. Heavy.

Formed near hot springs or in lavas associated with volcanic activity. Well-formed crystals are found in Almaden, Spain. Also found in Abbadia San Salvatore, Monte Amiata, Italy; Idria, Yugoslavia.

Identified by colour, weight and softness but may be mistaken for **realgar**. Cinnabar is the best source of mercury. It has been used as the pigment known as vermilion.

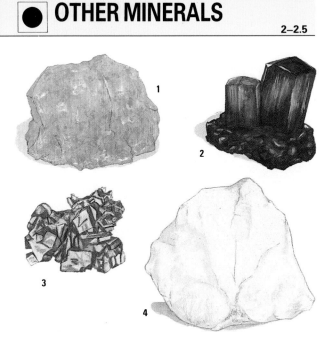

Glauconite (1)
Tiny, green, light crystals, perfect basal cleavage. Widespread. Cretaceous–Tertiary marine sands and silts. Forms diagenetically. Used in textiles, brewing, fertilizers.

Proustite (2)
Massive, striated, heavy. Fragile, shiny dark red crystals. Low temperature veins with silver. Erzgebirge, E. Ger.; Harz, WG; Sardinia, Italy. A beautiful, prized silver ore.

Acanthite-Argentite (3)
Heavy, malleable masses of shiny, lead-grey or black crystals. Occurs in veins with galena, silver. Lacks cleavage of galena. Weathers black unlike silver. Good crystals from Kongsberg, Nor.; Freiberg, E. Ger. Main ore of silver.

Kaolinite (4)
Friable, light, yellow brown or grey clay aggregate. Formed by hydrothermal alteration of feldspars. Widespread. Limoges, Fr.; Sardinia, Bavaria, Bohemia. Used in china clay, paper, medicines and cosmetics.

Colourless, white, yellowish or bluish. Crystals are usually large, well-developed short prisms. Also occurs in compact, earthy or encrusting form. Crystals lose water easily and turn white. Associated with halite and other borate minerals.

Transparent to translucent. Lustre glassy. Soft and light. Cleavage perfect in one direction, good in another. Brittle. Fracture conchoidal.

Rare in Europe outside Tuscany, Italy. Occurs in saline lakes and salt pans in desert regions as a result of evaporation. Up to 150 mm (6 in.) crystals are found in mud at Borax Lake and in Death Valley, California. Borax is mined commercially at Searles Lake, California, USA.

Borax dissolves in water and has a sweetish taste. It is unlikely to be confused with other minerals. Used as a flux in mining and may be a significant source of boric acid.

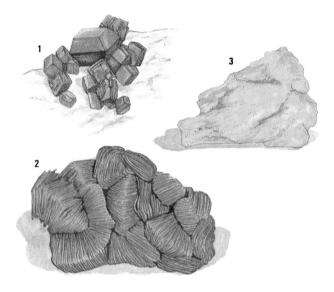

Found in radioactive pegmatites and sandstones. Derived from pitchblende (uraninite). They are striking yellow, orange or green minerals.

Tobernite (1)

Emerald green square plates or pyramids on quartz. Transparent to translucent. Lustre pearly to glassy. Perfect cleavage. Occurs in Cornwall, England; San Leone, Cagliari, Italy.

Autunite (2)

Greenish yellow square plates, micaceous flakes. Translucent. Perfect basal and prismatic cleavage. Found in pegmatite at Autun, France; Sabugel, Portugal; Lurisia, Italy.

Carnotite (3)

Bright yellow, soft powdery crusts. Lustre earthy. Abundant in sandstones in deserts. El Borouj, Morocco; Ferghana, USSR.

Colour light to dark green or black. Found as six-sided plates or foliated masses akin to mica, or may be granular or compact with slightly soapy feel. Chlorite (illustrated), chlinochlore, thuringite, penninite are well known minerals of the chlorite group.

Translucent. Lustre vitreous to pearly. Perfect platy cleavage, thin plates are flexible but inelastic. Massive varieties are easily carved and used for ornaments.

Occur as a filling in cavities in basalt; with albite and epidote in contact metamorphic rocks; with garnet in schist, amphibole and gneiss; also in hydrothermal deposits. Nice crystals occur at Zermatt, Switz., Val d'Ala (Turin), It.; Zillertal, Aus. Foliated masses occur throughout the western Alps.

Individual minerals of the chlorite group cannot easily be identified. Chlorite flakes, unlike those of **mica**, are flexible but inelastic.

Colour blue, bluish green or green; brown to black when impure. Does not form crystals. Commonly forms compact botryoidal masses, sometimes opal-like. Associated with malachite, azurite, limonite and cuprite.

Translucent. Lustre glassy, greasy or dull. Cleavage none. Very brittle. Fracture conchoidal. Streak white to pale bluish green.

Formed in the upper zone of copper deposits, mainly in arid regions. Large deposits occur in Morocco. Also found in the USSR and in Italy at Predarossa (Val Masino, Sondrio) and Monzoni in Val di Fassa (Trento). Chile is the main source.

Chrysocolla is much softer than **turquoise** or **chalcedony**. Its presence is an indication of some copper ores. It is used as an ornamental stone.

Colour lead grey. Crystals very common, occurring as cubic cleavage fragments or more rarely as octahedra. Also found in massive, granular or fine-grained fibrous forms. Occurs with quartz, barite, fluorite, pyrite, sphalerite, chalcopyrite, bornite and andradite.

Opaque. Lustre bright metallic. Cleavage perfect cubic, but obscured in extremely fine-grained material. Brittle, breaks up into cubes. Heavy.

Occurs in sedimentary rocks, hydrothermal veins and pegmatites. Found in the mines of Isle of Man, Derbyshire and Cumberland, England and in the ladinian limestone and Dolomites of Raibi, Salafossa, Gorno, Italy. Large deposits also occur in West and East Germany (Andreasberg, Harz; Freiberg, Erzgebirge).

Distinguished from **sphalerite** and **stibnite** by its perfect cubic cleavage and grey colour. The chief source of lead.

HALITE
den 2·5

2½

Colourless, white, reddish, yellowish or blue, often patchy. Crystals are cubes, sometimes with depresssions on each face. It also occurs in granular form, sometimes as large cleavable masses, as white crusts crystallized from volcanic gases or as the result of evaporation. Often found with gypsum.

Transparent. Lustre greasy or dull, warm and moist to the touch. Cleavage perfect, breaks into cubes. Brittle. Soluble in water.

Deposited from dried lakes by evaporation in saltwater basins. Forms massive sediments with clays. May flow under pressure and burst upward in weak places, forming plugs or domes. Occurs worldwide. Mined in Stassfurt, WG; Wieliczka, Pol.; Cardona, Spain; Salzkammergut, Austria; Lungro (Cosenza), Italy.

Easily recognized by the salty taste, perfect cubic cleavage and moistness. A vital ingredient of human and animal diets. Used in the manufacture of chemicals and food products.

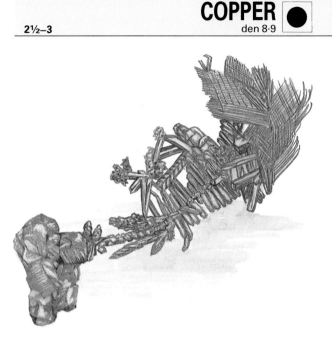

Colour rose or copper red on fresh surfaces, tarnishing brown to black, often with blue-green patches. Crystals rare, cubic, often flattened. Usually occurs as branching aggregates or in feathery form, scales, plates, lumps, often with traces of other metals. Associated with calcite, cuprite, zeolites.

Opaque. Lustre metallic. Cleavage none. Fracture hackly. Very ductile and malleable. The appearance of blue-green patches on rocks indicates the presence of copper.

Native copper commonly develops in basalt by the reaction of copper-rich solutions with iron minerals. Finest crystals and largest lumps come from the Keweenaw Peninsula, Lake Superior, USA. Crystals are found in Siegerland, WG, and Langban, Sweden. Small deposits are found near Pisa, Italy.

Because of its distinctive colour and malleability, copper is unlikely to be confused with other minerals. Widely used in alloys (brass, bronze), for ornaments, sculptures, utensils.

Colour greyish white, silvery, almost black when tarnished. Commonly occurs in feathery or wiry form, also found as scales, leaves, thin plates filling vein cracks or in massive form. Crystals very rare, cubes or octahedra. Occurs with calcite and barite or with other ore minerals.

Opaque. Lustre metallic. Cleavage none. Fracture hackly. Very malleable (may be hammered) and ductile (may be drawn into wires).

Widely distributed in basaltic rocks, in the oxidized zone of ore deposits or in hydrothermal deposits. Finest crystals occur at Kongsberg, Norway. Also found in Freiberg, E. Ger., and in Sardinia, Italy.

Acanthite/Argentite is a silver ore which tarnishes black and is frequently found with silver. Silver is often also present in small amounts in gold and lead-zinc ores.

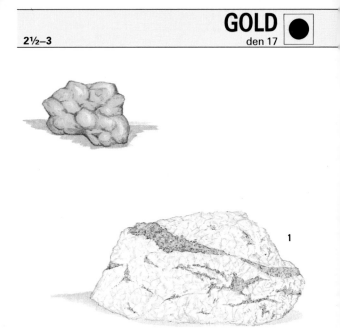

Colour gold yellow, brass yellow (depending on purity). Does not tarnish. Crystals distorted cubes or octahedra, in twinned aggregates or parallel groups. Also forms scales, grains, lumps, plates, leaves, wires. Usually contains silver and/or copper. Found with pyrite or arsenopyrite, often on quartz (**1**).

Opaque. Lustre bright metallic. No cleavage. Very heavy, malleable (may be hammered), ductile (may be drawn into wires).

Most gold occurs in quartz veins with pyrite and other ore minerals, also with scheelite and tourmaline. May also be "panned" from sedimentary deposits. Main global sources are all outside Europe, in S. Africa, USA, Canada and USSR. Once mined near Monte Rosa, It., and in Wales. Rhine alluvial placers.

Distinguished by untarnished golden colour, weight, malleability. **Chalcopyrite** is brittle, **pyrite** (Fool's gold) is harder and brassy, less heavy.

Colour dark lead grey, dull black when tarnished. Crystals are short prisms or tabular in shape, grooved on one face. They may appear six-sided or twinned in knee-like pairs. The mineral more commonly occurs in granular or compact form. One of the most abundant copper ore minerals.

Opaque. Lustre metallic, shiny. Brittle. Cleavage poor prismatic. Fracture conchoidal. Almost malleable, fairly heavy.

Found in ore veins in hydrothermal deposits and often associated with other copper minerals. Splendid pseudo-hexagonal crystals found in Cornwall, England. Found in Italy at Val di Cecina, Pisa; Libiola, Liguria and Calabona, Sardinia.

Distinguished from other copper minerals by its colour; it lacks the cleavage of **galena**. An important copper ore.

Jamesonite (3)
Dense mass of acicular or fibrous metallic grey-black crystals with basal cleavage. With galena, pyrite and calcite in veins. At St. Endellion, Eng.; Arnesberg and Wolfsberg, WG; Freiberg, E. Ger. A lead and antimony ore.

Bournonite (4)
Dense black-grey metallic massives of "cog-wheels" of fragile stubby tabular crystals with one perfect cleavage. With galena at Liskeard, Eng.; Harz, WG; Brosso (Turin) and Sardinia, It. Ore of lead, copper and antimony.

Anglesite (1)
Adamantine. Transparent, heavy tabular crystals of variable colour. Perfect cleavage. Alteration product of galena. Musen, Westphalia, WG; Anglesey, Wales. A lead ore.

Crocoite (2)
Hydrothermal alteration product of galena, source of chromium. Fragile, dense, orange-red acicular or granular crusts, greasy adamantine lustre. Found at Nontron, France.

1

Colour reddish bronze, surface readily tarnishes to iridescent deep blue and purple "peacock ore" (**1**). Crystals are rare, cubic or dodecahedral. Usually occurs in massive or granular form. May occur with pyrite, barite, calcite, andradite, galena, quartz, enargite, chalcopyrite or malachite.

Opaque. Lustre metallic, multicoloured. Cleavage poor, octahedral. Brittle. Fracture uneven.

Occurs in copper deposits, basic igneous rocks, pegmatites and hydrothermal veins. Nice crystals occur in Redruth, Cornwall, England; Salzburg, Austria and Vrancice, Bohemia, Czechoslovakia. Massive forms occur in Germany and Italy.

Identified by its distinctive colourful tarnish and the presence of other copper minerals. Perhaps the most important commercially mined source of copper.

Colour bright reddish orange, yellow or brown. Crystals are small six-sided prisms, sometimes hollow. It may also occur in fibrous form in radiating masses or as crusts. Associated with galena, crocoite, wulfenite and barite.

Transparent to translucent. Lustre shiny or greasy. Cleavage none. Brittle. Fracture conchoidal to uneven. Soft but very heavy. Streak white.

Formed in the alteration zone of lead deposits. Mostly found in Morocco and Mexico. Splendid large yellow, red and brown crystals occur in the Alps at Obir, Carinthia, Austria. Also found at Wanlockhead, Dumfries, Scotland.

Distinguished by colour from **pyromorphite**. A source of vanadium which is used in alloys and in dyes.

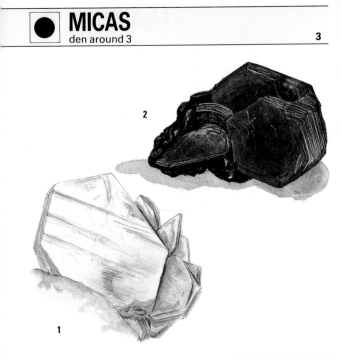

Colourless, white, amber, rose or pale green muscovite (**1**), dark green, brown or black biotite (**2**), yellow to brown phlogopite, mauve-purple lepidolite and others. Forms platelike, six-sided crystals, which are flexible, elastic, scaly or foliated. Also occurs as lamellar masses and minute flakes.

Perfect cleavage parallel to plates, breaking into very thin elastic sheets or scales. Transparent or translucent. Lustre pearly, even opaque looking through thin plates.

Widespread, micas are common in pegmatites. Phlogopite is associated with marbles. Large plates of muscovite come from Pizzo Forno, Switz. Lepidolite from Uto, Sweden, and Elba. Phlogopite from Pargas, Finland. Magnificent biotite crystals occur in geodes in the Vesuvius lavas, Italy.

The micas are distinguished from each other by colour and environment, from **chlorite** by the elasticity of their flakes.

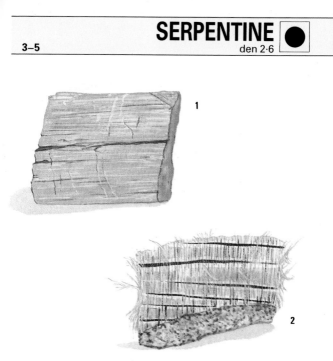

Colour green, yellow, brown, white or variegated. Occurs mostly in one of two forms. Antigorite (1) is compact, massive or botryoidal in form and used for building slabs, facings or carvings. Chrysotile (2) is fibrous asbestos, with flexible, tough fibres, used extensively in industry.

Translucent to opaque. Lustre silky, waxy, greasy. Fracture is conchoidal (antigorite), uneven or splintery (chrysotile).

Formed by the transformation of olivine and pyroxene and widespread in altered gabbros and ultrabasic rocks. Found at Val Antigorio, Piedmont, Italy. Also in Switzerland, Greece, Poland, Czechoslovakia and the Lizard Complex, Cornwall, England.

Softer than **amphibole** asbestos, but harder than **talc**. Named for the surface pattern in serpentinite rock.

CERUSSITE

den 6·5

3–3½

Colourless, white, grey, yellow or brown. Crystals are small and platy, may be grooved (**1**), and often form skeletal lattices (**2**). Occurs also as star-shaped groups or in massive, granular or compact form. Found together with galena, malachite, barite and smithsonite.

Transparent to translucent. Lustre adamantine. Cleavage prismatic, in two directions. Fracture conchoidal. Very fragile. Heavy.

This is a secondary mineral, usually formed from galena in hydrothermal replacement deposits. It has been found in Montevecchio, and Montepori, Sardinia, Italy; in Mezica, Yugoslavia and also in ores at Mechernich, West Germany.

Cerussite is an ore of lead and was once used as a white pigment.

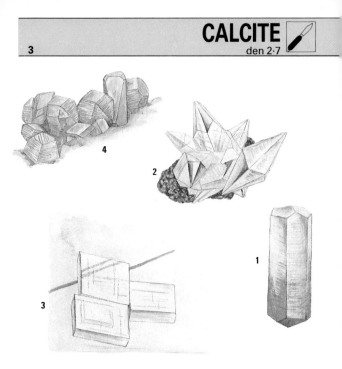

Very common, colourless or tinted crystals, very variable in size, thick tabular (Nailhead spar, **1**), Dogtooth spar (**2**), slender or needle-like, even microcrystalline in marble or chalk. Dissolves easily in dilute acid when bubbles are formed. Found with dolomite, siderite and magnesite.

Transparent to translucent. Lustre glassy, three cleavages nearly at right angles. Double refraction, as in Iceland spar (**3**). More easily scratched on base than on cleavages.

Found in sedimentary rocks like limestone or chalk often rich in fossils; in veins precipitated from solutions; in caves as stalactites or stalagmites; recrystallized as marble, travertine, banded as onyx marble. Widespread throughout Europe. Splendid crystals occur in Iceland, Italy and Germany.

Magnesite (**4**) is a closely related mineral with rhombohedral or prismatic crystals. Calcite is not easy to tell from brownish **siderite**, pink **rhodochrosite** or blue-green **smithsonite**.

Colourless or white, grey, yellow, brown, red and blue. Crystals usually tabular (**1**), thick or thin, often large or prismatic in form. Also occurs in featherlike groups, in granular, compact, lamellar or fibrous form. May form concretions like septarian nodules or desert roses (**2**). Occurs with apatite.

Transparent to translucent. Lustre glassy or pearly. Cleavage perfect basal and prismatic. For a light-coloured mineral, barite is very heavy.

Commonest in sedimentary rocks as concretionary nodules of free growing crystals, often in veins near sulphide ores. Widespread. Good crystals come from Westphalia, West Germany; Cumbria, Cornwall and Derbyshire, England; Trento, Como, Bologna and Sardinia, Italy.

May be identified by weight alone. **Calcite** and **fluorite** have different cleavages, **gypsum** is softer, **feldspar** much harder. Used in paper, cloth, paints, glass and oil drilling.

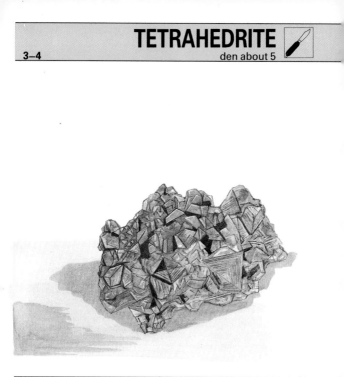

Colour steel grey to black. Crystals, as the name suggests, are rare tetrahedra, sometimes intergrown or twinned as parallel groups. Often occurs in massive, granular or compact form. Tetrahedrite is a member of a large group of minerals including tennantite.

Opaque. Lustre metallic. Cleavage none. Brittle. Fracture subconchoidal to uneven. Thin splinters of closely related tennantite may be deep red and translucent.

Tetrahedrite occurs in hydrothermal veins of copper, lead, zinc and silver minerals. Fine large lustrous crystals are found at Boliden, Sweden. Also occurs at Botes and Kapnik, Romania; Freiberg, E. Ger.; Schwatz, Austria and in Italy.

Distinguished from **sphalerite** by lack of cleavage. An important ore of copper, sometimes antimony, silver and mercury.

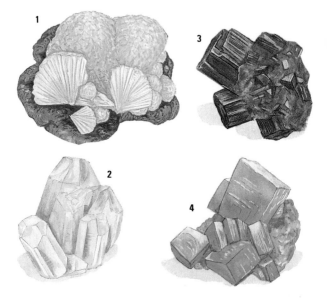

Adamite (1)
Colourless, yellow-green, blue, violet or light red vitreous, chunky tabular crystals with good cleavage. Also drusy crusts or ball-like aggregates. In oxidation zone of limestone ore deposits at Cap Garonne, France and Laurion, Greece.

Celestine (Celestite) (2)
Colourless, white, pale yellow-blue. In veins and sediments as nodules, fibrous masses or striated prismatic crystals. Transparent, vitreous. Perfect basal cleavage. Main ore of strontium, confused with denser **barytes**. Widespread.

Enargite (3)
An important copper-arsenic ore. Found as lamellar, black-grey, heavy, fragile, opaque aggregates with metallic lustre. Striated tabular crystals rare. Occurs with copper minerals in Bor, Yugo.; Baden, WG.

Wulfenite (4)
Heavy, yellow-orange tabular crystals. Adamantine. Translucent. White streak. Good cleavage. With cerussite, Bleiberg, Austria. Secondary Molybdenum ore.

3½–4   den 4·2

Colour golden yellow, readily tarnishing to iridescent or dark blue, purple and black. Crystals (**1**) are wedge-shaped, with uneven faces and may be grooved. Often occurs in massive (**2**) compact or granular form. Found most frequently with pyrite, chalcosine and gold but also with many other minerals.

Opaque. Lustre bright metallic with iridescent tarnish. Cleavage very poor. Brittle. Fracture uneven.

Widely distributed in various metamorphic rocks and hydrothermal deposits. Large 2 mm (¹⁄₁₆in) crystals are found in Savoie, France. Also occurs at Sulitjelms and Falun, Norway; Rio Tinto, Spain; Rammelsberg and Mansfeld, West Germany.

An important copper ore. Identified by hardness, colour and brittleness. **Pyrite** is paler, more brassy, harder and crystals are cubic. **Gold** is not brittle and does not tarnish.

Colour yellow, brown, green, deep red or black. Crystals are tetrahedral or dodecahedral, often with rounded faces; also occurs in granular, compact and botryoidal forms or as cleavage masses. Occurs with galena, fluorite, cerussite, arsenopyrite, pyrite, chalcopyrite, quartz and others.

Transparent to translucent, very dark varieties nearly opaque. Lustre resinous, nearly metallic. Cleavage perfect, in six directions. Brittle. Fracture conchoidal.

Found in same rock types as galena. Widespread. Superb large crystals occur in Trepca, Yugoslavia; Kapnik, Hungary; Pibram, Czechoslovakia; Alston Moor, England. Small fine crystals at Binnetal, Switzerland and Carrara, Italy. Also found at many zinc mines, e.g. Bleiberg, Austria and Raibi, Italy.

Can be mistaken for other minerals as its name (Greek for treacherous) implies. Identified by lustre and cleavage. The main source of zinc, widely used in industry.

Colour yellowish grey, pale yellow, light to dark brown, reddish brown. Crystals are rhombohedra with curved faces, sometimes grooved or tabular. Occurs in granular, compact, massive, botryoidal and fibrous form. Found with barite, chalcopyrite, calcite, rhodochrosite, galens and sphalerite.

Translucent. Lustre glassy, pearly or dull. Cleavage perfect rhombohedral in three directions. Brittle. Fracture uneven or conchoidal. Becomes magnetic when heated.

Occurs as large sedimentary deposits in shale, clay or coal seams; in ore veins and pegmatites. Fine crystals occur in Allevard, Isere, France; Styria, Aus.; Redruth and Camborne, Cornwall, Eng. Also as large sedimentary deposits in Lorraine; Bilbao, Sp.; Huttenberg and Herzberg, Aus.; Piedmont, Italy.

Distinguished from **sphalerite** by its rhombohedral cleavage. An important source of iron as it is free from sulphur.

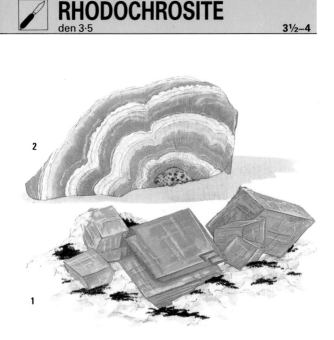

Colour pink, rose red, dark red, brown. Crystals rhombohedra or scalenohedra (**1**), often rounded. May also be granular, banded or massive (**2**) in form, or form botryoidal crusts or radiating aggregates. Occurs with chalcopyrite, galena and sphalerite, tetrahedrite and bornite.

Translucent. Lustre glassy or pearly. Cleavage perfect rhombohedral in three directions. Brittle. Fracture uneven, splintery. Streak white.

A common vein mineral, sometimes found in pegmatites. Occurs with silver, lead, zinc and copper ores at Freiberg, E. Ger. and Transylvania, Romania. Large deep pink crystals come from several mines in Ariege, France; Huelva, Spain; Ljubija, Yugo.

Identified by distinctive colour and cleavage. **Rhodonite** is harder and does not have the rhombohedral cleavage.

DOLOMITE

1

Colourless, white, pink, yellowish, greenish or grey. Crystals are usually rhombohedral with curved saddle-like faces (**1**). White to pinkish ones are associated with galena, sphalerite and calcite. Found also in granular, compact and massive forms. Also occurs as a rock.

Transparent to translucent. Lustre glassy or pearly. Cleavage perfect rhombohedral (in three directions). Brittle. Fracture conchoidal to uneven.

Found in limestone, as dolomitic limestone or dolomite rock, often near talc schists, serpentinites, pegmatites. Widespread. Fine crystals occur at Brosso-Traversella, Piedmont, Italy; Binnetal, Switzerland; Freiberg, E. Ger.; Cornwall, England and Navarra, Spain.

Its crystals are much less common and smaller than **calcite** and never form scalenohedra. Used as a building or ornamental stone and in industry. Ankerite is the iron rich variety.

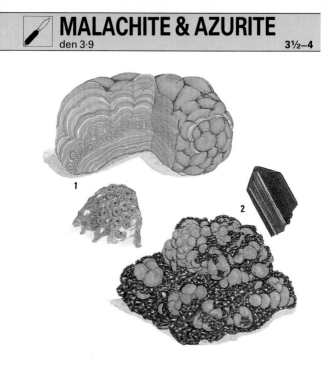

Malachite (**1**) is emerald, grass or dark green. Rare crystals are stubby prisms or radiating silky needles. Usually occurs in botryoidal form with concentric colour bands and alternating layers of azurite. Azurite (**2**) is light to deep blue or black, with large equant or tabular crystals.

Translucent. Cleavage perfect in one direction. Brittle. Lustre of massive malachite dull. Azurite crystals glassy. Fracture of malachite conchoidal, of azurite subconchoidal.

These two copper minerals always occur together. Most common in the weathered zone of copper deposits at Chessy, Lyon, France. Also found at Laurium, Greece; Betzdorf, WG; Sardinia, Italy.

Colour and colour banding of malachite is distinctive. Other blue minerals are harder than azurite. Now used as decorative and ornamental stones when polished and once used as pigments.

Colour ruby red or reddish black. Crystals are octahedra, cubes or combinations of these. Often occurs as intergrown needles, sometimes as coatings on native copper or in cavities; may also be massive in form. Nearly always associated with other copper minerals like malachite (**1**) or azurite, and with limonite.

Translucent to transparent. Lustre submetallic, bright. Cleavage poor octohedral. Brittle. Fracture conchoidal.

Forms near the surface of copper deposits as a result of weathering. Fine specimens occur at Chessy, Lyon, France. Also found in Monsol, France; Redruth and Liskeard, Cornwall, England; Westphalia, WG; Sardinia and Libiola, Liguria, Italy.

Important copper ore. Mostly identified by its associations. Some clear red crystals have been cut as gems. **Zincite**, which may also be red, never occurs with copper minerals.

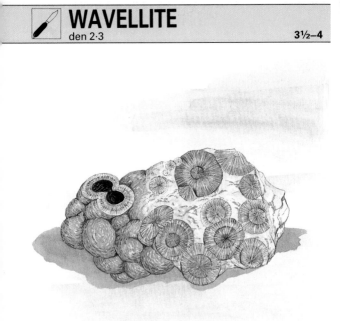

Colour white, grey, yellow, pale green, brown. Crystals prismatic, rare. Usually forms radiating fibrous spherules, rosettes and botryoidal crusts, or encrusting earlier-formed minerals. Associated with quartz, muscovite, turquoise and limonite.

Transparent to translucent. Lustre silky. Cleavage not apparent in fibres. Brittle. Fracture uneven, splinters easily.

Formed at low temperatures and found in fissures of rocks rich in aluminium as well as in some phosphate beds. Found in quantity as yellow-green spherules at Barnstaple, Devon, Eng. Also found in Kinsdale and Clonmel, N. Ireland; Frankenberg, Saxony, WG.

Botryoidal crusts of wavellite may be confused with **chalcedony**, but are much softer. Wavellite may be used in fertilizers.

Colourless, green, yellow-green or brown. Crystals are stubby six-sided, usually hollow, prisms or may be barrel-shaped. Also found as aggregates, in massive form or as crusts. Occurs with vanadinite and the closely related, rare mimetite, as well as with barite, cerussite and galena.

Translucent. Lustre dull or greasy. Cleavage none. Brittle. Fracture irregular. Very heavy.

Formed in the weathered zone of lead ore deposits. Beautiful green crystals occur in Cornwall, England and Pribram, Czechoslovakia. Excellent material is found at Clausthal-Zellerfeld, Harz Mountains, WG and Leadhills, Scotland.

Identified by the colour and shape of the hollow crystals, their dull lustre and lack of transparency. A minor ore of lead sought after by mineral collectors.

ARAGONITE

den 2·9

3½–4

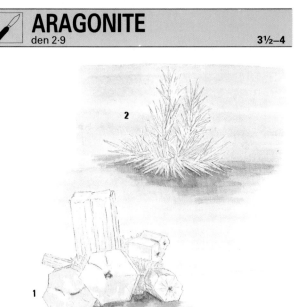

Colourless, white, yellow, brown, pale green or violet. Crystals often form twins or triplets (**1**), resembling six-sided prisms but for the grooves on their base. Aragonite may also occur as needles (**2**), as long or short prisms, as fibrous or columnar masses, or it may form concretions.

Transparent to translucent. Lustre glassy to resinous. Brittle. Fracture subconchoidal. Cleavage good in one direction, poor in two others.

Occurs in hot spring deposits (in travertine), in ore veins with gypsum and calcite where it is precipitated from solutions. The skeletons of many organisms often consist of aragonite. Found at Bastennes, Fr.; Molina de Aragon, Sp.; Alston Moor, Eng.; Styria, Aus.; Sicily and Vesuvius, It.

When heated, aragonite changes to calcite. **Calcite** has three intersecting cleavages and forms differently shaped twin crystals.

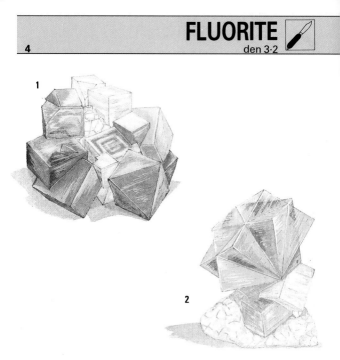

Colourless, white, blue, green, purple, yellow, brown or bluish black. Crystals are cubic in form, often colour-zoned (**1**), frequently found as penetration twins (**2**), rarely as octahedra. Occurs with cassiterite, topaz, tourmaline and apatite or with barite, quartz and sulphide ores.

Transparent, brittle. Lustre glassy. Perfect octahedral cleavage in four directions. Fracture conchoidal.

Found in pegmatites and hydrothermal veins with lead-zinc-silver sulphides. Widespread. Pink cubes occur at St. Gotthard, Switz.; pale green octahedra at Kongsberg, Nor. Purple and colourless cubes occur on galena in Cumbria and Derbyshire, Eng.; yellow crystals at Wolsenberg, WG.

Identified by cleavage, cubic crystals and hardness. **Calcite** is softer, **quartz** much harder. Chinese fluorite carvings are marketed misleadingly as green quartz.

Zincite (1)
A collectable zinc ore. Massive, distinctive dark red to orange-yellow, heavy, granular, adamantine crystals with perfect cleavage. In contact metamorphic deposits at Bottino, Tuscany, Italy and in Spain and Poland.

Wollastonite (2)
Fibrous, acicular or radiating masses of white crystals with pearly lustre and good cleavage. In calcareous contact metamorphic zones and low pressure regional metamorphism. Brittany; Pargas, Finland; Black Forest, WG.

Manganite (3)
Ore of manganese. Long, black deeply striated crystals. Medium-heavy, metallic, with perfect cleavage. A low temperature hydrothermal deposit with calcite, barytes at Ilfeld, Harz, E. Ger.

Wolframite (4)
Main ore of tungsten. In hydrothermal veins, granite pegmatites and contact metamorphic rocks. Dense, black-dark grey, metallic, prismatic crystals with one cleavage. Black to red-brown streak. Dartmoor, England.

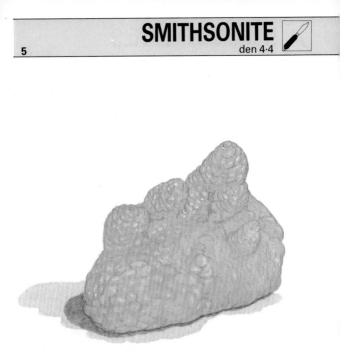

Colourless, green to apple green, blue to bluish green, brown or yellow. Crystals indistinct, rounded rhombohedra. More often it forms botryoidal masses but may also be compact or granular in form or produce incrustations. Associated with galena, cerussite, malachite and azurite.

Translucent. Lustre glassy to pearly. Cleavage perfect rhombohedral in three dimensions. Brittle. Fracture uneven, splintery.

Occurs in the upper zone of massive hydrothermal deposits. Found in lead mines in Turkey, USSR and the Alps (Udine, Raibi). Beautiful blue-green material occurs at Santander, Spain and Laurium, Greece. Slightly paler yellow material is found in Sardinia, Bergamo and throughout Italy.

Identified by its botryoidal form and colour. Sometimes an important ore of zinc. Harder and heavier than **calcite**, **magnesite** or **rhodochrosite**.

HEMIMORPHITE
den 3·4

4½–5

1

Colourless, white, blue green, yellowish or brownish. Crystals usually small, thin plates; they may also form blades, divergent groups or fan-shaped aggregates. Occurs also in massive (**1**), botryoidal and granular forms. Associated with smithsonite, gypsum, hematite and calcite.

Transparent to translucent. Lustre glassy. Cleavage perfect prismatic in two directions. Brittle. Fracture uneven to conchoidal.

Formed at low temperatures in lead and zinc deposits. The finest crystals occur at Moresnet, Belgium; Cumberland and Derbyshire, Eng. Also occurs at Olkus, Poland; Carinthia, Austria; Raibi and Udine, Italy.

A source of zinc. Best identified by its thin bladed crystals. **Smithsonite** is heavier.

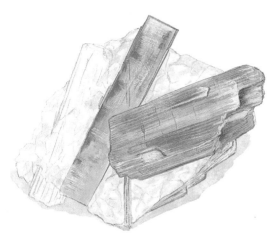

Colour blue, also green, white, grey, yellow, pink, blackish. The distribution of the colour may be patchy. Occurs as long bladed crystals. These may be isolated or in aggregates, and they are usually embedded in rock.

Transparent to translucent. Lustre glassy. Cleavage perfect. Fracture splintery. Hardness variable, a pocket knife will scratch crystals parallel to length but not across width.

Found in schist and gneiss formed from clay-rich rocks. Splendid blue crystals with staurolite at Pizzo Forno, Switzerland. Also found in Morbihan, France; in Tyrol, Austria; Val di Vizze and Val Passiria, Bolzano, Italy.

Used as a refractory, for porcelains, high temperature bricks and spark plugs. Unlikely to be confused with any other mineral.

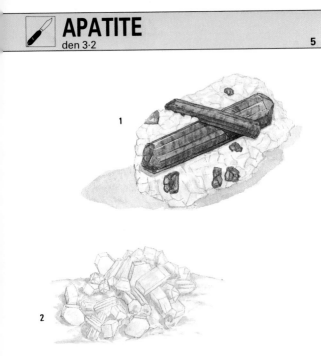

Colourless, green, brown, yellow, violet, pink or red. Crystals common, short or long six-sided prisms (1), often tabular (2). Also found in massive, granular or compact forms. Occurs in many rocks with titanite, magnetite, nepheline, aegirine, andradite, phlogopite or with albite and mica.

Transparent to translucent. Lustre glassy or greasy. Cleavage poor, parallel to base. Brittle. Fracture uneven, conchoidal.

Widespread in plutonic rocks, pegmatite dykes, bedded sediments, contact metamorphic rocks. Tabular blue crystals from Knappenwand, Austria; famous violet crystals from Ehrenfriedersdorf, E. Ger.; clear crystals from Laachersee, W. Ger. Large masses at Alno, Sweden and in Italy.

Often confused with other minerals but **beryl** is harder, **tourmaline** prisms are grooved and not six-sided. Apatite is a major consituent of bone.

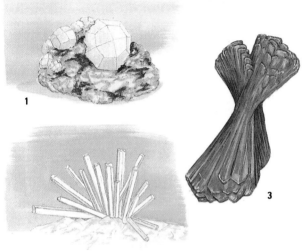

1

2

3

Minerals in this group are closely related in composition and occur in the cavities of basalts. They can lose their water content, replacing lost water without a change in their crystal structure.

Analcime (1)
5–5½. Colourless, white or greenish. Trapezohedral crystals line cavities in basalt. Iceland; Cyclopean Islands (Sicily).

Natrolite (2)
5–5½. Colourless or white needles or radiating masses. Transparent to translucent. Good prismatic cleavage, uneven fracture. Found in Puy-de-Dôme and in Antrim, N. Ireland.

Stilbite (3)
3½–4. White, grey or reddish brown sheaf-like bundles, unique among zeolites. Transparent to translucent. Perfect cleavage. Found on Isle of Skye, Scotland and in Iceland.

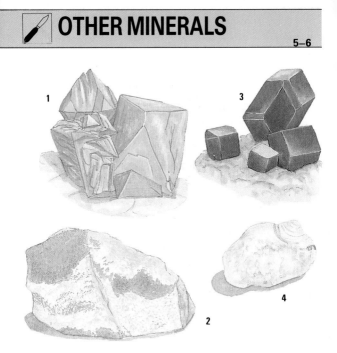

Scheelite (1)
Yellow, green or reddish grey.
With cassiterite, wolframite in
pegmatites and hydrothermal
veins. Heavy, adamantine,
pseudo-octahedral crystals. .
Good cleavage and white streak.
Cornwall, England; Zinnwald,
E. Ger.; Traversella, Italy.

Turquoise (2)
Light, massive, pale blue, with
perfect basal cleavage and waxy
lustre. Result of weathering of
aluminium-rich igneous rocks.
St. Austell, Cornwall, England;
Messbach, Saxony, WG.

Dioptase (3)
Vivid emerald-green stubby
rhombic crystals. Highly prized.
Good cleavage, adamantine
lustre. Found with other copper
minerals. Baita, Romania.

Opal (4)
Varies from milky-white
"Geyserite" to blue-black
"precious" or reddish "fire".
Amorphous crusts and veins, no
cleavage, greasy lustre.
Cervenica, Czech.; Caernowitza,
Hun.; Geysir, Iceland.

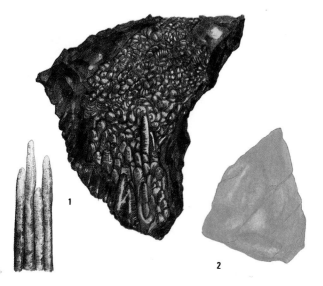

Colour yellow, yellow-brown, reddish brown to black. Crystals rare prisms with vertical grooves. Usually forms botryoidal masses (**1**) with a radially fibrous internal structure or may be platy, earthy, columnar or bladed.

Opaque, very thin slivers transparent. Lustre dull, silky to metallic. Cleavage perfect in one direction, imparting a soft greasy feed. Fracture splintery. Streak orange brown.

Formed by the weathering of iron minerals or precipitated directly in marine lagoons or freshwater bogs (bog iron). Large deposits are mined in Alsace-Lorraine, France and in Westphalia, WG. Bladed crystals occur as rosettes in Thuringia, WG and Cornwall, Eng.

The main constituent of ochres and limonite (**2**), a mixture of iron minerals. It is an important iron ore, distinguished from **hematite** by its streak colour and its structure.

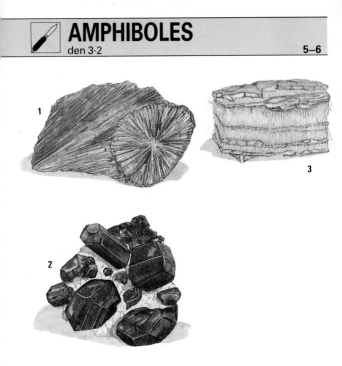

Members of this widespread group of rock-forming minerals occur as elongated or stubby prisms, fibres or aggregates. Fibres may be matted and asbestos-like. Tremolite is colourless to white, actinolite (**1**) bright to dark green, hornblende (**2**) green, brown or black. Crocidolite (**3**) is fibrous.

Transparent to translucent. Lustre glassy. The two good prismatic cleavages intersecting at an angle of 120° are diagnostic. Fracture subconchoidal to uneven or splintery.

Tremolite-actinolite occurs in metamorphosed limestone, gneiss, serpentine schist throughout Alpine Europe. Hornblende is very widespread: Greiner, Zillertal, Aus.; Pernio, Pargas, Fin. Riebeckite occurs in schists in Galicia, Sp. Crocidolite (blue asbestos) in Framont, Vosges and glaucophane in Groix, France.

The angle between cleavages in **pyroxenes** is 90° and its crystals are more stubby. **Tourmaline** has no cleavage. **Jadeite** (the other jade mineral) is much harder and more valuable.

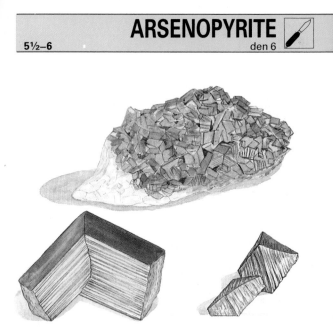

Colour silver white to steel grey. Crystals are common, elongated prisms with grooved faces; spear-shaped twins (**1**) are common. Also occurs in columnar, granular, compact or botryoidal form. Associated with quartz, chalcopyrite and gold; occurs in pegmatites with garnets and plagioclase.

Opaque. Lustre metallic. Cleavage distinct, prismatic. Brittle. Fracture uneven. Sparks form and it smells of garlic when struck with a hammer.

Formed at moderate to high temperatures, in gold-quartz and/or cassiterite veins, in some metamorphic deposits. Fine crystals are found at Boliden, Sweden; Freiberg, E. Ger.; Cornwall, England; Sulitjelma, Norway; Valle Anzasca, Novara, Italy.

Best identified by the shape of its crystals. Mined not so much for its arsenic content as for its by-products of gold, silver and cobalt.

FELDSPARS
den 2·7

6

Colourless, white, pink, grey or green prismatic or tabular crystals, often large (in granite, pegmatite, porphyry, gabbro), sometimes twinned. Also as small grains of white or pink orthoclase (1) mixed with white or grey albite and/or green microcline (2) producing a texture in rock known as perthite.

Transparent (in sanidine) to translucent. Lustre glassy. Fracture conchoidal. Usually two good cleavages. Group includes orthoclase, microcline, albite, labradorite, anorthite and sanidine.

Principal constituents of most igneous and metamorphic rocks; orthoclase occurs at Baveno, Italy and Karlsbad, Czech.; microcline on Sardinia, albite in W. Alps of Switz. and Aus. Labradorite comes from Norway and has bluish reflections used in carvings. Sanidine is common on Elba and Sicily.

Amazonite, a green microcline, is used for jewellery and ceramic glazes. **Calcite** is much softer and more soluble than feldspar. Harder **quartz** has no cleavage.

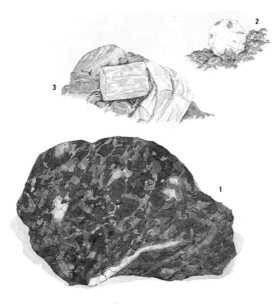

Colour white, grey, blue, violet, greenish, even pink. Crystals are rare dodecahedra. Usually occurs in large masses (**1**), also found in compact, nodular or granular form. Normally found with nepheline and also with leucite. An attractive ornamental stone.

Transparent to translucent. Lustre glassy or greasy. Cleavage poor, dodecahedral in six directions. Brittle. Fracture uneven to conchoidal.

Occurs in deep-seated igneous rocks, especially in syenite pegmatites. Monte Summa and Mt. Vesuvius, Italy; Langesund, Norway; Laachersee, WG. Found with leucite-nepheline on Vesuvius and the Alban Hills, Lazio, Italy.

The rich blue colour of massive sodalite is characteristic. Leucite (**2**) occurs only in lavas. Nepheline (**3**) has three perfect cleavage planes and greasy lustre.

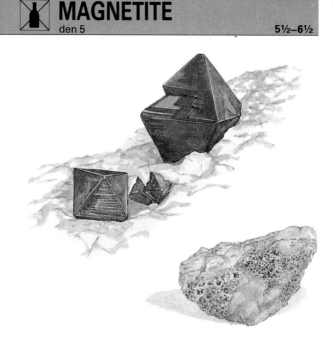

Colour black. Crystals perfect octahedra, rarely dodecahedra or cubes, with grooved faces, sometimes twinned. Also occurs as compact and granular masses with bluish iridescence. May occur with andradite, talc, calcite, chlorite, barite and fluorite.

Opaque. Lustre metallic. Cleavage none, only poor octahedral parting (in four directions.) Brittle. Fracture uneven. Strongly magnetic (natural lodestone.) Streak black.

Abundant, occurs in a number of igneous, sedimentary and metamorphic rocks. Huge deposits occur at Kiruna, Norway. Splendid crystals are found at Binnetal, Switz.; Pfitschtal, Aus.; Val di Vizze, Bolzano and the volcanoes of Lazio, It.

Distinguished from other iron minerals by its strong magnetism and black streak. Spinel is a related mineral, that forms similar but harder crystals. Red ones may form gem stones.

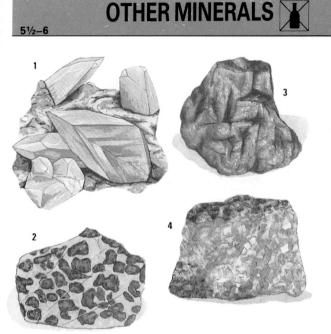

Sphene/Titanite (1)
Wedge-shaped brown, grey-green, yellow or black crystals. Adamantine. Two good cleavages. White streak. In granites, at Tavistock, Devon, England. In gneiss and schist at Arendal, Norway.

Chromite (2)
Principal ore of chromium. Black granular masses of octahedral crystals. Heavy. No cleavage, even fracture, opaque, metallic, dark brown streak. In peridotite, serpentinite and placers. France and Ramberget, Norway.

Niccolite/Kupfernickel (3)
Important nickel ore. Massive, pale copper-red, tarnishing grey-black. Metallic. No cleavage, pale brown-black streak. Freiberg, Saxony.

Rhodonite (4)
Deep pink granular or fibrous masses veined with black manganese oxides. Tabular crystals rare. Medium density, vitreous, translucent. Perfect 90° cleavage. In contact metamorphism of impure limestones. Langban and Pajsberg, Sweden. Prized for jewellery.

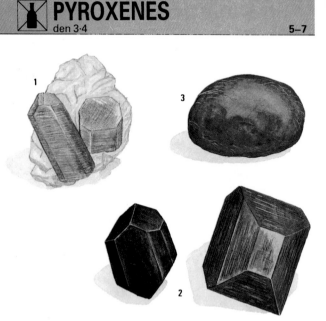

Diopside (**1**) is common as large white, light to dark green, or brown crystals with octagonal cross section, embedded in marble. Augite (**2**) occurs as green, brown or fine black crystals or may be granular or massive. Aegirine is fibrous. Jadeite (**3**) occurs as waterworn boulders or felted masses.

Translucent to opaque. Lustre vitreous. Fracture uneven or splintery. Two perfect prismatic cleavages intersecting at nearly 90° are diagnostic. Jadeite is the hardest pyroxene.

Widespread, diopside occurs in hornfels marbles in Zillertal, Aus.; Nordmarken, Switz. and in Italy. Augite is common in gabbro, perdotite, pyroxenite, basalt, volcanic rocks on Vesuvius, Etna, Stromboli, Italy, and in Auvergne, France. Jadeite and aegirine are rare.

Distinguished from **amphiboles** by almost rectangular cleavage. Nephrite jade is softer. **Tourmaline** has no cleavage, nor has **olivine** which, unlike diopside, is never found in marbles.

SCAPOLITES (Wernerite)

5–6½   den 2·6

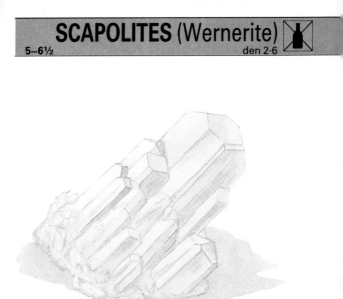

A series of minerals which range from Meidnite to Marialite. Often occur as prismatic tetragonal prisms with strong vertical striations or as fibrous-granular masses. Exhibit variable colours ranging through white, blue, grey, pink, violet, yellow, red. White streak.

Transparent to opaque. Lustre vitreous to pearly. Subconchoidal fracture. Distinct cleavage.

Mainly metamorphic minerals occurring in contact altered impure limestones and skarns and regionally metamorphosed schists, gneiss and amphibolite. Also found in pegmatites. Found in central Alps around Lake Tremorgio, Switzerland; Mt. Somma, Pianura, Naples and on Elba, Italy.

Identified by occurrence, white streak and form. Can be distinguished from **zeolites** by hardness. A rock-forming mineral of interest to scientists and collectors. Gemstone varieties.

Colour yellowish to olive green. Often occurs as stubby prismatic embedded grains, or solid granular masses (**1**). Individual crystals (**2**) are rare and mostly already altered to serpentine. Olivine is the common name for a family of minerals which includes forsterite and fayalite. Peridot is gem quality olivine.

Transparent to translucent. Lustre vitreous. Brittle. Fracture conchoidal, uneven. Cleavage indistinct, in two directions at right angles.

Essential mineral of gabbro, peridotite, basalt. Dunites contain 90% olivine. Occurs in some metamorphic limestone. Never found in rocks with free quartz. Found in basalt porphyries, in Mourne Mts., N. Ire.; Vesuvius lavas, It.; Forstberg, WG. Peridots occur in Zebirget, Egypt and Fayal, Azores.

Identified by colour and occurrence. Of other green minerals, **epidote** has one perfect cleavage, **grossular** has none, **apatite** is softer, **tourmaline** does not occur in gabbro or basalt.

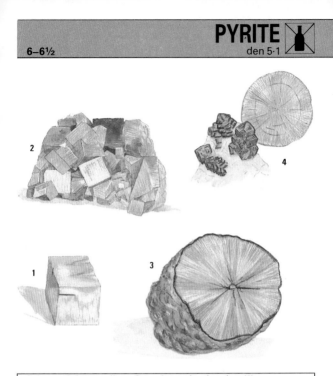

Colour pale brass yellow. Crystals are simple cubes (**1**) or pentagonal dodecahedra with grooved, curved faces, often intergrown (**2**). Octahedra, when present, are very smooth and shiny; often occurs in massive or granular form or as concretionary masses of fine radiating needles (**3**).

Opaque. Lustre metallic. Cleavage none. Brittle. Fracture uneven. Pyrite often replaces fossils.

Occurs in all types of rock, hydrothermal deposits and veins associated with gold, chalcopyrite. Widespread. Large crystals occur at Rio Tinto, Spain; Sulitjelms, Norway; Falun, Sweden. Pyritohedra at Rio Marina, Livorno, Italy. Striated cubes are found at Gavarrono, Grosetto, Italy.

Known as Fool's Gold because it resembles **gold**, which is much heavier, softer, not brittle and not grooved. Marcasite (**4**) is a similar, related mineral with paler, arrow-shaped crystals.

Colour golden to reddish brown, red, brown or black. Crystals usually long, slender, grooved prisms or needles; twins may be knee-shaped (**1**) or form rosettes. Also occurs in granular or massive form. Very fine golden to reddish hair-like needles often occur in crystals of quartz (**2**).

Translucent to transparent, large crystals nearly opaque. Lustre strong, metallic. Cleavage distinct prismatic. Brittle. Fracture uneven.

Formed in plutonic and metamorphic rocks and hydrothermal deposits. Crystals occur at Graz, Austria and St. Gotthard, Switzerland; with apatite in Norway. Needles are found in quartz at Travetsch, Switzerland.

Identified by characteristic shape and lustre of the grooved crystals. Commercial ore of titanium, used in pigments. **Cassiterite** is heavier, less shiny, and not grooved.

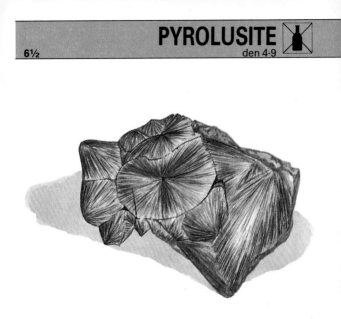

Colour steel grey to black. Usually occurs in soft massive, fibrous, columnar, divergent or radial forms or in granular or powdery masses. Crystals, which are prismatic, are very rare. Associated with barite, hematite, calcite and other manganese minerals.

Opaque. Lustre metallic to dull. Cleavage perfect prismatic. Brittle. Fracture uneven. Streak bluish black. Only the crystals are hard.

Found in veins, sedimentary and hydrothermal deposits. The most widespread of all manganese minerals, but collecting places are few. Occurs in Restormel, Cornwall, England and Platten, Bavaria, WG.

Only good crystals may be recognized, otherwise impossible to distinguish from other manganese minerals by eye. Used in steel alloys and by the chemical industry.

Colour brown, yellow, reddish brown, almost black, sometimes in bands. Crystals commonly short square prisms, sometimes pyramids, often forming knee-shaped twins. Also as rounded pebbles "stream tin", or in botryoidal form with concentric banding, or as a radiating fibrous structure, "wood tin".

Transparent to translucent. Lustre greasy to dull. Cleavage distinct prismatic. Fragile. Fracture uneven. Heavy.

Typically found in pegmatites and hydrothermal veins, but the largest deposits are sedimentary. Fine crystals occur at Le Villeder, Morbihan, France; Erzgebirge, E. Ger. Mined in Cornwall, England. Also occurs in veins on Elba and in pegmatites at Piona, Lake Como, Italy.

Distinguished from other minerals by its weight. This was the main source of tin which was used for bronze making in ancient times.

Colourless, brown, green, grey, yellow, red, bluish. Crystals are short square prisms with pyramidal ends, or bipyramids. Also occurs as lumps or grains in beach sands. Associated with orthoclase, biotite, albite and amphibole.

Transparent (gem quality) to translucent. Lustre usually high and diamond-like, but can be dull. Cleavage poor prismatic in two directions. Brittle and hard. Fracture conchoidal. Heavy.

Common in granite, syenite, pegmatite and some limestones. Low-grade crystals come from Tyrol, Austria; the German Rhineland; Loch Garvee, Scotland and southeast Norway. The main source is Travancore, India.

Identified by weight, hardness, square cross section. Heavier than **vesuvianite**. Gem quality transparent stones may be obtained by heating but they may lose their colour in time.

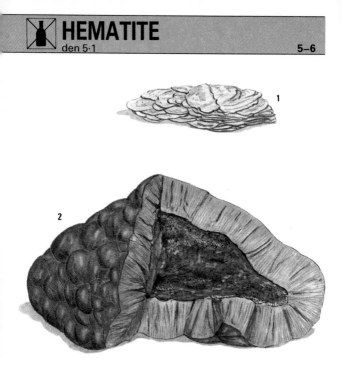

Colour grey, red, reddish brown or black. Crystals thick or thin six-sided plates, tablets or rosettes but well developed crystals are rare. Also occurs as lens shaped scales (**1**), kidney-shaped masses (**2**), in botryoidal, micaceous or earthy (red ochre) forms. One of the commonest minerals.

Opaque. Lustre metallic to dull. Cleavage none. Brittle. Fracture uneven, splintery. Very thin plates may be translucent and red. Streak bright to dark red. Weakly magnetic.

The main deposits are of sedimentary origin but hematite is present in many igneous rocks and lavas. Beautiful black crystals occur on Elba and in Cumbria, England. Iron roses are typical of St. Gotthard and Binnetal, Switzerland.

The main iron ore even though **magnetite** is richer. Its characteristic red streak and colour distinguish it from other ores and iron-bearing minerals.

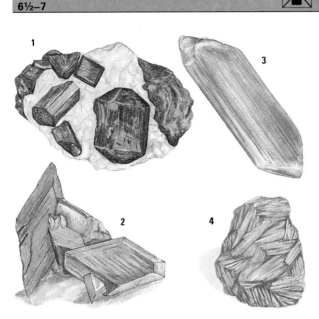

Idocrase/Vesuvianite (1)
Stubby prismatic crystals with pyramidal terminations. Brown, olive green, yellow. Conchoidal fracture. Opaque, vitreous, characteristic white streak. In contact metamorphic skarns with garnets. Vesuvius, Italy; Norway.

Axinite (2)
Characteristic violet-brown wedge-shaped crystals. Vitreous, colourless streak. In contact metamorphic rocks at Bourg d'Oisans, Isère; Cornwall, England. Used in jewellery.

Spodumene (3)
An important lithium ore. Rod-like striated, white, yellow, grey, pink or green crystals. Translucent, vitreous. In lithium-bearing pegmatites in Scotland and Norway.

Sillimanite (4)
Long, grey, brown, pale green crystals or fibrous masses. Transparent, vitreous, with one perfect cleavage. In high temperature regional metamorphic rocks and pegmatites of Bohemia; Bavaria and Saxony, WG.

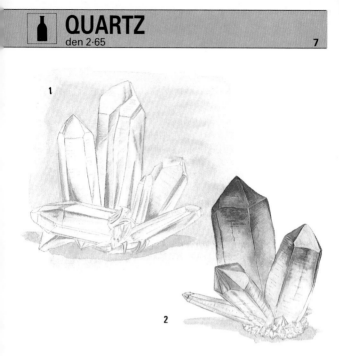

Colourless (rock crystal, **1**), white (milky quartz), pink (rose quartz), yellow (citrine), purple (amethyst, **2**), brown-black (smoky quartz). Forms six-sided prisms ending in large and/or small rhomb faces, or may be granular, disseminated, even massive in form. Tiger eye has yellow-brown asbestos fibres.

Lustre glassy or greasy. Usually no cleavage. Fracture conchoidal. Horizontal striations on prism faces. Hard. Often has inclusions of mica or hematite flakes as in aventurine.

An essential constituent of granite, felsite, diorite, pegmatite, sandstone etc., present in rhyolite, contact metamorphic rocks, gneiss, schist and veins. Citrine occurs in Dauphine, France. Smoky quartz occurs in the Cairngorms, Scot. Milky and colourless rock crystals are common in the Alps.

Colourless **beryl** is harder with a poor cleavage and no grooves. **Feldspars** are softer with good cleavage. **Topaz** is harder with good cleavages. **Fluorite** is softer than amethyst.

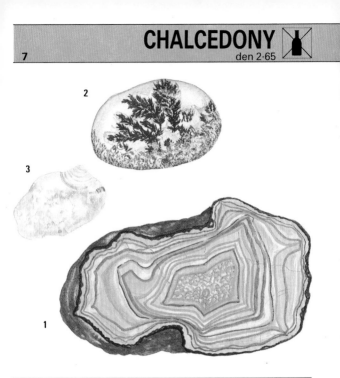

A microcrystalline bluish or variously coloured compact variety of quartz. Found as nodules (1) or botryoidal crusts. Forms apple-green chrysoprase, reddish brown carnelian and sard, dark green, red-spotted bloodstone, colour banded agate (2), black-white banded onyx, flint in chalk or chert.

Transparent to translucent. Lustre glassy, dull or waxy. Brittle to tough. Fracture conchoidal.

Chalcedony forms microcrystalline precipitates. Occurs in hydrothermal deposits, as amygdales in basalt in Iceland. Coloured agates come from Idar-Oberstein, WG; chrysoprase and jasper from Tyrol and Saxony; onyx from Turkey.

Opal (3) is a closely related gemstone mineral that is softer than **quartz** and does not form crystals. It has a pearly lustre, dissolves in water and occurs as veins or globules.

Colour yellow or all shades of green to brownish black; very common. Its long slender grooved prisms are often terminated by two slanting faces. Found as thin pale crystalline crusts or in granular or massive form. When rotating the prism and looking through it, its colour changes from green to brown.

Transparent to translucent. Lustre vitreous. Cleavage perfect, parallel to length of prism. Brittle. Fracture uneven.

In altered igneous and metamorphic rocks, pegmatites, contact metamorphosed limestone. Remarkable dark green crystals are found at Untersulzbachtal, Austria. Fine crystals occur at Bourg d'Oisans, Isère, France; Arendal, Norway.

Colour and appearance are very characteristic. **Actinolite** has two cleavages intersecting at 120°, **tourmaline** has no cleavage. Neither has the prominent colour change when rotated.

STAUROLITE

1

Colour yellowish brown or reddish brown to black. Forms prismatic crystals with six-sided cross-section. Two individual prisms are frequently intergrown (twinned) at 60° or 90° producing a regular cross (**1**). Grey when weathered. Associated with albite and biotite.

Translucent to opaque. Lustre glassy or dull. Cleavage poor, parallel to length of crystal. Brittle. Fracture uneven to subconchoidal.

Occurs in schist and gneiss of metamorphosed rocks. Beautiful single crystals occur at Aschaffenburg, Bavaria; Milltown, Inverness, Scotland and Killiney, Dublin, Eire.

Staurolite is easily recognized by colour, shape and mode of occurrence. The associated, but rare, sillimanite has same composition, but occurs in fibrous masses embedded in rock.

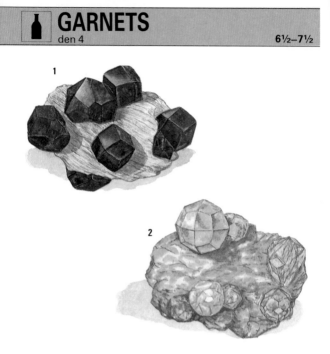

There are several closely related garnets. They are wine-mauve red almandine (**1**), yellowish red pyrope, purplish red spessartine, colourless, yellow to pale green grossular (**2**), brownish red-black andradite, and emerald green uvarovite, easily recognized by their rounded, 12-sided crystals.

Transparent to translucent. Lustre glassy. Fracture uneven or conchoidal; sometimes granular. No cleavage, sometimes indistinct parting.

Pyrope occurs in peridotite in Ticino, Switzerland. Almandine is found in diorite or with andalusite in Norwegian hornfels. Grossular with vesuvianite is found in limestone of the western Alps; spessartine in pegmatite and blue schist; andradite in pegmatite or skarns; uvarovite in serpentinite.

Clear varieties are widely used as gemstones; pyrope is used as an abrasive in garnet paper. Their crystal shape is characteristic. **Apatite** is softer and **zircon** heavier.

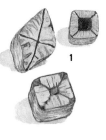

Colour white, grey, pink, brownish, olive green. Occurs in granular form or as stubby crystals, nearly square in cross-section. Cigar-shaped prisms embedded in schist with cross or checkered pattern in cross-section are chiastolite (**1**). Found with quartz, biotite, corundum, almandine, topaz, cordierite.

Transparent to translucent. Lustre glassy, dull when altered. Two good cleavages intersecting at 89° and 91°. Fracture uneven to subconchoidal.

Found in granite pegmatite with quartz, microcline, muscovite; contact metamorphic rocks with corundum; in schist and gneiss with almandine and cordierite; in hydrothermal deposits with topaz and pyrophyllite. Crystal: Andalusia. Chiastolite at Salles de Rohan, Morbihan, France.

Used as a gemstone and in ceramics. Cut stones exhibit two colours: green on the sides and reddish brown on the ends. Distinguished from **tourmaline** by square cross section.

TOURMALINE
den 3·2

7–7½

Colour black (**1**), pink and red (rubellite, **2**), brown, green or multicoloured, often colour-zoned (**3**). Crystals long or short prisms with rounded triangular cross section, the two ends with different terminal faces. Also found in columnar form or as radiating needles with spodumene and andalusite.

Transparent (when it may be of gem quality) to opaque. Brittle. No cleavage. When a prism is rotated, the colour visibly changes.

Occurs in granite pegmatites, schists and hydrothermal deposits. Red, blue and green gem quality crystals (rubellite is the most valuable) occur with large colour-zoned crystals at San Pierro, Elba. Black crystals are common on Dartmoor, Devon, England; Spittal, Austria and Kragero, Norway.

Readily identified by curved triangular cross section, grooved prisms, absence of cleavage. Harder than **apatite**. **Beryl** and **apatite** are not grooved. A widely used semi-precious stone.

Colour pale to dark blue, violet, grey, brown, black. Usually occurs in massive or granular form. Crystals are rare. May occur with andalusite, almandine, corundum, biotite. Because it so readily alters to chlorite or muscovite, fresh material is rare.

Transparent to translucent. Lustre glassy. Cleavage poor. Brittle. Fracture conchoidal to uneven. When a crystal is turned its colour changes from blue to grey.

Usually associated with aluminium-rich metamorphic rocks, such as schist, gneiss, hornfels and also found in volcanic rocks. Massive cordierite occurs in Tuscany, Italy. Finest crystals come from Bodenmais, Bavaria; Orijarvi, Finland.

Identified by colour and colour change. The clear blue variety is sometimes used as a gemstone.

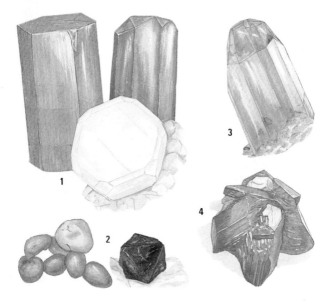

Beryl (1)
Emerald, Aquamarine, grey,
white, yellow. Opaque, vitreous,
light, hexagonal prisms in
granite pegmatites and high
temperature veins. Elba and
Craveggia, Italy. Main source of
Beryllium.

Spinel (2)
Variable, often red, pink, white.
Opaque, vitreous, small
octahedrons with poor cleavage,
white streak. Twins common. In
granulites and contact
metamorphic dolomites and
ultramafic rocks. Monte
Somma, Vesuvius, Italy.

Topaz (3)
Variable, often yellow or
colourless. Prismatic, vitreous
translucent crystals with one
cleavage. In granite pegmatites
and high temperature mineral
veins on Elba and Sardinia, Italy
and in Cornwall, England.

Chrysoberyl (4)
Variable, often honey-yellow,
brown, colourless. Adamantine,
translucent prismatic crystals
with good cleavage. Pseudo-
hexagonal twinning. In
pegmatites and mica schists at
Marsikov, Czech.; Norway;
Italy.

Colour pink, red (ruby, **1**), blue (sapphire, **2**), violet, brown (**3**), grey, black with magnetic impurities (emery). Crystals are six-sided tabular or short prismatic, rough, rounded, barrel-shaped. Faces may be grooved, repeated twinning is common. Also in massive or granular form (emery).

Transparent to translucent. Lustre glassy. No cleavage, only a parting resulting in grooves. Brittle but very tough and hard. Fracture uneven to conchoidal.

Formed in syenite, pegmatite, metamorphic rocks. Found in gravel and sand. Low quality grey corundum occurs at various places in Vercelli and Piedmont, Italy. Emery is mined at Naxos and Samos, Greece and Smyrna, Turkey. Crystals can be found in France, Norway and Sweden.

Identified by hardness and weight, only **diamond** is harder. Ruby and sapphire are highly valued gemstones. Sapphire may contain inclusions giving a star-like effect in cut stones.

The hardest known mineral. Like graphite, made of pure carbon but with a different atomic structure. Usually colourless, also yellow, brown, grey, green, black and blue. Crystals are often small rounded octahedrons.

Transparent. Adamantine lustre with a very strong dispersion of light. Perfect cleavage.

Found in situ in decomposed olivine-rich kimberlite in South Africa, USSR and India. Widespread in river placer deposits. No known European source.

Colourless gemstone varieties account for less than a quarter of diamonds found. The vast majority are used as high quality expensive abrasives.

ORGANIC MINERALS

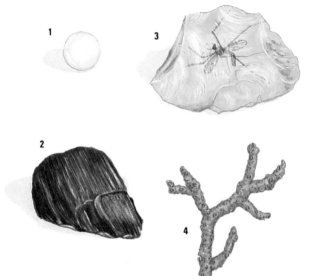

Pearl (1)
Product of freshwater and
marine bivalve molluscs that are
not true oysters. Mainly
aragonite, with organic material.
Freshwater pearls found in
Scotland. Marine pearls in Red
Sea, Persian Gulf.

Jet (2)
A fossil wood with the
composition of impure coal.
Black, vitreous with a
conchoidal fracture. Very light.
Combustible. Aude, France;
Asturias, Spain; Whitby,
England.

Amber (3)
A brown, yellow, white or green
fossil resin. Very light.
Originated as resin from *Pinus
succinifera* in the Tertiary era.
Found in Baltic Europe.

Coral (4)
A calcium carbonate mineral
produced by coral polyp
skeletons. Variable colour: red,
pink, blue and white. Found in
the Mediterranean.

Index and Check-list

Keep a record of your findings by ticking the boxes.

CRYSTAL TYPES

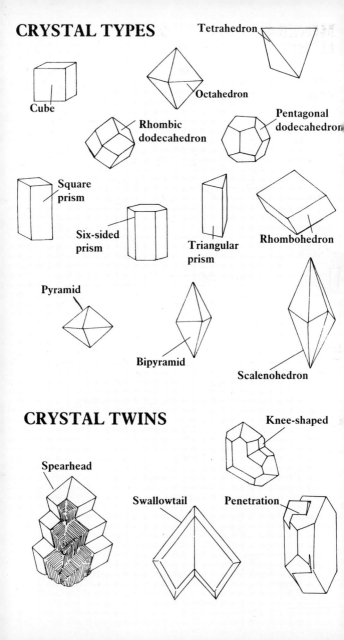

Tetrahedron

Cube

Octahedron

Rhombic dodecahedron

Pentagonal dodecahedron

Square prism

Six-sided prism

Triangular prism

Rhombohedron

Pyramid

Bipyramid

Scalenohedron

CRYSTAL TWINS

Knee-shaped

Spearhead

Swallowtail

Penetration